P9-BZG-765

CONTENTS

This Is Your Time

It was a test we could all hope to pass
But none of us would want to take—
Faced with the choice to deny God and live,
For her there was one choice to make.
This was her time,
This was her dance;
She lived every moment,
Left nothing to chance.
She swam in the sea,
Drank of the deep,
Embraced the mystery
Of all she could be—
This was her time.

Though you are mourning and grieving your loss,
Death died a long time ago.
Swallowed in life, so her life carries on;
Still, it's so hard to let go.
This was her time,
This was her dance;
She lived every moment,

Left nothing to chance.
She swam in the sea,
Drank of the deep,
Embraced the mystery
Of all she could be.

What if tomorrow?
What if today?
Faced with the question,
Oh, what would you say?
This is your time,
This is your dance;
Live every moment,
Leave nothing to chance;
Swim in the sea,
Drink of the deep;
Fall on the mercy
And hear yourself praying,
"Won't You save me?"

"This Is Your Time" written by Michael W. Smith and Wes King. © Copyright 1999 Milene Music, Inc. (ASCAP), Deer Valley Music (ASCAP), Sparrow Song (BMI), and Uncle Ivan Music (BMI). All rights on behalf of Sparrow Song and Uncle Ivan Music administered by EMI Christian Music Publishing. International rights secured. All rights reserved. Used by permission.

CHAPTER 1

THE LONGEST DAY

I WAS LAYING down the final tracks for an album when I got a phone call that rocked my world.

Debbie, my wife, said, "Something's going on in Colorado. There's been a shooting, and I think some kids may have been hurt. You might want to turn on the TV and see what's happening."

I'm not a "news junkie." In fact, I've canceled my newspaper subscription twice for a simple reason: I get tired of bad news. It's hard not to get apathetic and numb when you read story after story of tragedy. I care about what's going on in the world, but sometimes you can only take so much.

But Debbie knows that kids have always had a special place in my heart. If young kids are involved, I'm interested, so I stopped recording and turned on the news. Virtually every station was carrying the story live.

Somebody was shooting up a high school in Littleton, Colorado.

At that point, still early in the day, nobody knew

exactly what was going on. I watched in horror as kids streamed out of Columbine High School with their hands above their heads. The early eyewitness reports were chilling: kids had seen their classmates shot and left to bleed, and the police were still unable to enter the school. My heart just about stopped when one student answered unequivocally, "Yes, there are dead kids in the school."

Unbelievable, I thought. *This is just unbelievable. Here we go again.*

The shootings took place on a Tuesday. Little did I know that three days later I'd get a call from Colorado's Governor Owens, who wanted to know if I'd sing at a memorial service for the slain kids.

Initially, I was shocked that the governor asked me, but I was eager to do all I could to help the teens at Columbine work through what had happened. But then I remembered a couple of conflicts, and my heart sank. I didn't see how it could work out. My son Tyler's birthday was on Sunday—the same day as the memorial service—and on top of that, I had already committed to speak at a local church for a bunch of kids.

I don't miss my kids' birthdays, so I told Michelle,

my assistant, that as much as I'd like to attend the Columbine memorial service, I just couldn't. Though I realized this was a good opportunity to inject some faith and hope in a tragic situation, it didn't seem right to walk out on my previous commitments to Tyler and the church.

But God had other plans.

"AMBASSADOR" SMITH

I hadn't been asleep for more than a couple of hours Friday night when I woke up and felt like the Lord was telling me, *You're my ambassador, and I want you to go to Colorado. Your previous commitments will take care of themselves. People will understand.*

I lay awake for some time afterward, mulling over what I thought I had just heard. While I don't discount the possibility of God speaking into my heart, I don't believe I can trust all my impressions, either. If this really was God talking, a few things would have to play out. First, Tyler would have to give me his okay. After all, he was the one who would be asked to make the biggest sacrifice. And second, the church kids would have to give their okay.

At breakfast, I pulled Tyler aside and said, "Tyler, you understand what's just happened in Colorado, don't you?"

"Yeah, I know about it, Dad."

"They've asked me to come and sing at the memorial service this weekend. Initially I said no, because it would mean missing your birthday party tomorrow, but I think God wants me to go. Before I'll even consider going, though, I want to make sure it's okay with you. We can still pull out all the stops for a family party on Monday, but it will mean my missing the party with your friends on Sunday."

"That's okay, Dad," Tyler said. I know him well enough that I can read his eyes, and he was sincere. It really didn't bother him. Even at the young age of eleven, he understood the importance of what was taking place.

"We'll blow it out on Monday—have a big party, okay?"

Tyler smiled.

Next, I phoned one of the leaders of the youth group I was supposed to speak to. I explained the situation, and she was incredibly understanding. "It sounds like you should go to Littleton, but you've got to make that call," she said.

When I phoned back a little later and said, "I really think I'm supposed to do this," she answered, "We *all* feel like you need to go."

I put down the phone, amazed at how easy everything had gone. Suddenly, I realized something that was a little bit sad, a little bit daunting, and a little bit confusing.

I was going to Colorado.

THIS IS A DREAM

We left early Sunday morning. Amy Grant joined me and my manager, Chaz, on the flight out.

"Are you ready to do this?" I asked Amy.

"I think so," she replied. I think both of us felt a bit inadequate for what lay before us. I wondered, *Who am I to comfort a parent who has lost a kid? I have no idea what that's like.*

But for some reason, God wanted me there. He had worked everything out, and I was eager to do whatever it was He wanted me to do.

Amy and I spent most of our time going over the

information we had been given about the kids and the teacher who had been wounded and killed in the shooting. It was sobering to realize that I'd meet some of the survivors who were still in the hospital, as well as parents of the kids who had been killed. I kept asking God, *What am I going to say?*

Two state policemen picked us up at the airport and brought us to the mall where the memorial service was going to be held. They had set up a stage behind a movie theater. The parking lot surrounding the stage was massive; you could see forever.

I hoped to see several people, especially Cassie Bernall's and Rachel Scott's parents. Both of these teens had been believers, and reports had said that Cassie—and perhaps Rachel also—had been asked about her faith before she was shot.

"Do you believe in God?" Cassie had been asked.

"Yes," Cassie had answered.

That was her last word, as one of the killers then coldly took her life.

The individuals speaking or performing at the memorial were given their own "theater," where parents and teens could meet anyone they cared to. Vice President Al Gore had his theater, Franklin

Graham had another one, and Amy and I were in one together. I looked down the hall and saw people start to line up. The weird thing was how silent it was. This was unlike any gathering I had ever experienced. These parents had just lost their kids, something I can't even imagine having to deal with, so I didn't know quite what to expect. The grief was just so apparent, and there wasn't a thing I could do about it.

It was all so surreal. *This is a dream,* I kept telling myself. *This isn't really happening. You're not really here. This tragedy hasn't really happened.*

Chaz broke into my thoughts by touching my arm and saying, "Cassie's mom and dad are here; they want to say hi to you."

I walked over to Cassie Bernall's mom, wanting with all my heart to comfort her. She stretched out her arms to greet me as if we were long-lost friends, and I'm somewhat embarrassed to admit that *I'm* the one who lost it. Something broke deep inside me. I started weeping while Misty held on to me. The reality of her loss hit me so hard.

"It's okay, it's okay," Misty said.

I finally said, "I'm so sorry." Misty thought I was

talking about her losing Cassie—which I was sorry about—but I was also sorry about the fact that *I* was supposed to be comforting *her*, and now it was the other way around! Here was Misty, patting my back as I wept onto her shoulder, telling me everything was going to be okay.

I knew then that I had met some special parents.

Misty's husband, Brad, shook my hand. Their son, Chris, shook my hand as well. He seemed to be reeling, having a hard time accepting his sister's death—which I completely understood. I could only imagine what it would have been like to lose my sister, Kim, at Chris's age.

There, in the midst of that theater, I was impressed by an incredible sense of peace radiating from Misty. Such peace could come only from God. Where I expected to see anguish and even accusation or bitterness, instead I saw an almost angelic courage and acceptance that caught me totally by surprise. I had never seen a grief-stricken woman who managed at the same time to radiate such a deep peace. It was an unbelievable sight.

That was my first clue that there was more to this Columbine story than what had been reported in the papers and on TV. Misty's demeanor injected my uncertain heart with hope and strength. I realized that though Satan had done a horrible, tragic thing, God hadn't forsaken the people of Littleton. Seeing God's peace flowing from this woman, and the favor He had shown to this family, was a great encouragement. Somehow, I knew that millions of lives would be challenged by Cassie's story. I was certain that in some way God would use this family's grief to encourage others—and that's exactly what has happened. I didn't know then that Misty would write a book that would sell hundreds of thousands of copies, telling the story of how Cassie had been transformed from a rebellious teen into a courageous Christian martyr, but I knew that somehow, God had special plans for this family.

I also got to meet Rachel Scott's parents. Rachel's story was as dramatic as Cassie's. Rachel had actually shared the gospel with Dylan Klebold and Eric Harris just three weeks before the shooting. She urged them to consider Jesus Christ. According to various accounts, Rachel was first shot in the leg. A second bullet pierced her backpack and knocked her onto the ground.

One of the gunmen walked over to Rachel, who was now facedown on the ground but still alive, and picked up her head by her hair.

"Do you still believe in God?" he asked.

With tremendous courage, Rachel used what little life she had left to whisper, "You know that I do."

A second later, Rachel was immediately with the Lord.

At the theater, Rachel's dad, Darrell Scott, hugged me and said, "Rachel loved your music."

I'm still surprised when people tell me this, but in this context, I was almost knocked over. For some reason, I felt an immediate connection with Rachel and grieved the loss of her life, even though I had never met her.

All this added to the surreal feeling that shrouded the entire day.

"I'm so sorry," I told him, again not realizing the awesome things that God had planned for Rachel's dad. Darrell would eventually travel across the country, speaking words of grace and hope to many. Rachel's death created a powerful ministry of evangelism and challenge to the Church. Darrell often reads from Rachel's diary when he speaks, and virtually everywhere he goes, a hundred or more kids come up and commit or recommit their hearts to the Lord.

DOING THE DAVID THING

After Rachel's dad spoke, it got eerily quiet, creating a real awkward situation. Then Amy did something brilliant. She walked over to her guitar, picked it up, and started quietly singing a hymn, "I Surrender All."

One by one, we were all mesmerized. Something almost mystical happened when she started to sing. The grief never left, but it was covered with a grace and assurance that took away some of the sting.

Amy's doing the David thing, I said to myself. David ministered to Saul with music, and I've been in many similar situations where music was the perfect balm. It was really sweet; Amy's music transcended the gap that words alone could never overcome. I was tremendously proud of Amy, particularly of how she ministered to people in grief like it was the most natural thing in the world.

It was good preparation for what was to follow.

CLOSED EYES

We walked into the service, and I greeted a few familiar faces, including my good friend Franklin Graham. He was bold in his talk and delivered a strong message.

When one hundred bagpipes started playing "Amazing Grace," I took Amy's hand. I cried off and on through the program, but every time there was a particularly touching moment, I found myself instinctively reaching out and taking Amy's hand again, especially when they started reading aloud the names of the kids who had died and released a dove into the air after each name. The whisper of the doves' wings, flapping wildly as they sought air, was eerily reminiscent of a young life stretching its way toward heaven.

Finally, the time came for me to sing. Normally, I don't get too nervous when I perform. I've played in front of presidents, television audiences numbering in the millions, and live packed houses, so I've gotten used to being on stage. But for a couple of reasons, this performance felt different. First, and most importantly, I was looking out at relatives who had lost loved ones. I was singing to grieving parents, hurting brothers and sisters, distraught aunts and uncles, anguished grandparents, and confused classmates.

Second, I was moved by the fact that I could see 75,000 grieving people, many of them kids. For some reason, my eyes were drawn to the red-eyed teens, holding on to each other in their sorrow, trying to be brave and get through this service.

I started singing "Friends" and kept telling myself, *You've got to get through this, Michael.* If you watched the service, perhaps you noticed that my eyes were closed most of the time. That's because I had to focus on just getting the song out.

If I forgot and opened my eyes momentarily, I saw another weeping teen, so I closed my eyes again. *Michael,* I reminded myself, *don't look.* When you're singing and you feel really sad, your throat can close up, so I had to be careful. When I finally got to the last line, "a lifetime's not too long, to live as friends," my eyes opened and fell immediately on Cassie Bernall's parents.

That's when I lost it.

VAL

After the service, the sprinkling rain was an appropriate response to our collective grief. God Himself seemed to be weeping. A sea of people flowed down the street, many laying flowers at little makeshift memorials. Some cars owned by kids who had been killed were now virtual shrines. People from around the world had sent tokens of their sympathy. John Tomlin's Chevy was so covered by flowers and gifts that you couldn't even see the truck. (John was a committed believer who had traveled to Mexico with his dad to build a house for the poor.)

Now it was time to meet the wounded. I was already emotionally wasted from the service, so I had mixed feelings about meeting the survivors. On one hand, I wanted to meet these kids and encourage them, but another part of me wondered how much more I could take.

Within minutes the hospital tour taught me a lesson I won't soon forget. I never realized before how much punishment the human body can take and still survive. These kids were horribly assaulted, yet their spirits were strong, and they were pulling through with heroic courage. It was particularly tough seeing some kids who, realistically, shouldn't have survived. Their bodies were riddled with gunshot wounds, but somehow they had pulled through.

We walked into one room where a young woman named Anne Marie lay unusually still. We talked briefly. She was in good spirits and even managed to smile, though it was clear that she was seriously injured. After we left, a nurse pulled me aside and said, "I didn't want to tell you this before you went in, but she's just found out she's paralyzed for life. She'll never walk again."

That was it. I disappeared into a corner and shut down. I couldn't go on until I spent a few moments regaining my composure. (Just as I was finishing this book, I called Anne Marie. There's now movement in her legs, which is a miracle in itself. Doctors are calling this "an extremely good sign.")

But I still had more people to visit. The next person I saw was Valeen Schnurr, who also had been asked about her faith before she was shot. Val had been studying in the library (where Cassie was killed) when the gunmen broke through and started shooting. Seconds later, Val was slammed in the side with thirty-four shotgun pellets.

"Oh God, oh God, don't let me die!" she had cried out.

One of the shooters had been just an arm's length away. In a weird moment, he had stopped the killing, looked at Val, and asked, "Do you believe in God?"

Val, knowing that these boys were on a devilish rampage, still said yes. Miraculously, the gunman's attention had been diverted as he reloaded, and Val had survived to tell her story.

Val's injuries were so serious that she had two operations just to get the pellets removed. She also suffered through numerous sessions of plastic surgery to repair the physical scars. I was amazed by her strength and vibrancy when she greeted us. She was, without a doubt, the most upbeat of all the students we met. Her faith inspired all of us.

Val's attitude was a definite pick-me-up. I was so glad I went to her room, because I needed the inspiration after such a long day. Once again, I went in there intending to comfort someone else, only to find that I was the one who received comfort.

After we left Val's room, it was time to leave.

One of the most emotional days of my life was coming to an end.

SOMETHING NORMAL

On our way to the airport, I couldn't get the stories and tragedies out of my mind. I couldn't forget the faces of kids who had faced more grief and terror than I've ever known. I couldn't close my eyes to the images of parents who realized they'd never see their children graduate, get married, or have kids. I couldn't forget how many of the kids we met in the hospital would be scarred for life because of just a few hours of hatred let loose.

It all seemed like too much chaos and too much evil, even for this fallen world. I craved something normal, something to bring me back out of the surrealistic fog that kept me weighed down. I couldn't remember the last time I had eaten anything, and my body felt totally depleted. But even more than that, I craved something that was ordinary, part of everyday life, something to bring me out of the crazy, mixed-up world I had just walked through.

Believe it or not, we stopped at a McDonald's. It

was the only normal thing that happened to me that day. I rarely eat at a McDonald's anymore—because of Deb's influence, I try to eat a lot better than that—but this day, I needed the most "normal" American experience I could find—and McDonald's had it, for less than four bucks. I got the most normal sandwich—a Big Mac—and surrounded it with the usual fries and Diet Coke.

Nobody said much on the flight back home. Our heads were swimming with the personal stories and memories that would mark all of us for the rest of our lives. When the plane landed, I got into my car. Suddenly all alone, I lost it once again and cried all the way home.

Deb saw a broken husband walk through the door. I was devastated, and she knew it. She wanted to love on me, but she realized this was something that God and I had to work out, so she wisely left me alone and let me weep really hard.

I just needed to cry it out.

CHAPTER 2

BE GLORIFIED

THE TYPE OF grief I experienced at the memorial service wasn't the kind that passes away like the morning fog. It hung on like a season. No matter what I did, I just couldn't get Cassie Bernall off my mind. Her martyrdom haunted me—in a good way. I was inspired by her courage and fired up by her commitment to her faith even in the face of death. I couldn't help asking myself, *Would I have said yes? If I had a loaded gun pointed at my head, and knew that saying yes would mean the end of my life, would I have been as faithful as Cassie?*

And then I lost myself in prayer. "Oh, God," I prayed, "be glorified. Somehow, through all this horrible tragedy, Lord, somehow, *somehow,* make Your name glorified. Please make some good come out of this."

One of the reasons Cassie's story touched me so deeply is because I really love kids. Even though I'm in my early forties, my personality and actions still make me feel like a kid sometimes! When we go to people's homes, the kids usually end up in one room and the adults in another—except for me. I'm usually with the kids. I think I'll still be a kid when I'm eighty. I may not be able to move very fast then, but if the kids will let me, I'll still want to hang with them!

Another reason Cassie's story impacted me so much is that I believe there are thousands of kids on the edge—walking that gray line, straddling the fence, trying to decide which field they're going to live in. I believe that God has given me the role of an ambassador to round up the troops: "Come on, guys, it's time to jump over to God's side and get serious about your faith."

We act as if life will go on forever; many kids think they have another several decades to decide how they'll live their lives. But the tragedy at Columbine reminded all of us that that's a lie; none of us know how long we have left.

One of the ways I can reach young people is through my music, so a song about Cassie's ordeal seemed an obvious route to take. I picked up my guitar, but for some reason, felt reluctant. I didn't want anybody to think I was taking advantage of a terrible tragedy. It's not that I sit around and worry all the time about what others think of me, but I wasn't sure people would understand the true intent of my heart. Most wouldn't know what I had been through, how a national tragedy had become a very personal ordeal.

In spite of my initial hesitation, I just *had* to write the song. When I am tremendously moved by something, as I was by Cassie's story, it usually finds its way into my music.

Composing the music didn't take long; it came together in about five minutes. That was actually a good sign. Usually I do my best work this way. The tune was inspired in large part by that amazing sense of peace that Cassie's mom, Misty, had shown to me at the memorial service. Of all the events that sad day, that's what stuck with me most.

After I had the music down, I called Wes King. This was unusual. I haven't worked with Wes much, and this song was unusually close to my heart, but I believe that God was guiding Wes and me together. I filled him in on the memorial service and my meeting with Cassie's and Rachel's parents. As we talked, one theme kept pressing itself onto us. It was almost like the words were written in heaven. We tried other thoughts, but kept coming back to "This is your time."

That was the theme that eventually prevailed.

Wes delivered the song lyrics less than a week later. We had to tweak the words for the next week and a half, getting the chorus right and the end of the verses to come together. I believe that Wes has written life-changing lyrics that will be around long after he passes away. Certain songs last a lifetime, and I think this is one of them.

SACRED GROUND

Several weeks went by before I mustered the courage to play the song for Cassie's parents. I realized I was treading on sacred ground, and the last thing I wanted them to think was that I was trying to benefit from the death of their daughter. But finally I called Misty and told her, "You know what? I don't need to put this song on the record. I want you to hear it, though; if you don't want me to include it on my next album, I won't." I would definitely have honored her request, either way.

Misty and I met at a home in Beaver Creek, Colorado, where my family spends a lot of time together. My parents were there, and the Bernalls—who just happened to be in the mountains—drove over and spent the day with us. After we talked for a while, Misty said, "I really want to hear 'This Is Your Time.'"

I put in the rough cut CD and could see the fresh emotions welling up as Misty and Brad relived the significance of their daughter's life and death. The last note was still hanging in the air when Misty proclaimed, "I love it!"

Tears flowed freely; there wasn't a dry eye in the living room. Apart from my own, those were the first tears shed after a song that would have far more play than I realized. I couldn't have imagined at that time what the song could do or where I would be asked to play it.

I came back to Nashville, confident of the song's potential but still believing that something was missing. It just didn't end right. Obviously, people were reacting to it, but—though it's difficult to describe this—I sensed that it needed an additional spiritual element. How could I evoke this? What instrument could I use?

I went to sleep with the problem in my head, then woke up in the middle of the night and heard bagpipes. You need to realize that I *never* wake up in the middle of the night. With five kids, I've learned to sleep hard. I lay in bed and rewrote the song in my head.

Two weeks later, we had a bagpipe troupe come in and play on the track. Those of us working on the record sat there in awe. Adding the bagpipes took the song to a whole new level. I truly believe that this was a God thing. I've *never* used bagpipes on an album before.

Writing "This Is Your Time" wasn't like writing a pop song. It's not too often that you can add one instrument and make such a dramatic change. But this song has a message like few other songs I've written. Though I didn't know why, there seemed to be a spiritual significance in this change.

I called Misty to tell her about the change—I figured it was her family's song as much as mine—and heard her gasp.

Oh no, I thought. *Have I done something wrong?*

"You're not going to believe this," Misty said.

"What?"

"Cassie loved bagpipes. They were her favorite instrument."

A holy quiet followed. My knees got weak, and I stood in awe of God.

You know what? I don't think the bagpipes were a coincidence. Somehow, God had translated a young woman's heart into a song that could inspire a generation.

CHAPTER 3

LITTLE CHOICES

YOU WOULDN'T BE human if you lived through something like the Columbine shooting and didn't ask God, *Why?* Why was Cassie's miraculous journey from darkness to light cut so tragically short? Why did courageous young women like Val Schnurr and Rachel Scott have to face such terror? Why were other kids scarred or even paralyzed for life?

But now I move past that question a lot faster than I used to. In fact, it now appears that there is little explanation (beyond the miraculous) for why the entire school didn't blow up, killing hundreds of kids instead of twelve. Klebold and Harris shot at two twenty-pound propane tanks. Officials say the tanks should have exploded, but they didn't, and there isn't a single "expert" who can explain why.

Instead of questioning God, I asked questions of the Church. We lost a battle, no doubt about it. We lost a bunch of kids who shouldn't have been lost. That made me angry! But instead of railing against God, I cried out, "Wake up, Church! We're losing our calling! We're not taking responsibility for our children! Why aren't we reaching the Dylan Klebolds and the Eric Harrises?"

I've got one answer: two guys that full of hatred, anger, and evil would never have set foot inside most church outreach programs. There is no denying that what Dylan Klebold and Eric Harris did was hideous and cruel. Their actions were undeniably evil. They were certainly seething in anger. These two young men were devoid of faith and choking on their bitterness, and they bear the responsibility for choosing to continue in that lifesyle. As history now proves, they were two accidents waiting to happen, but I still believe with all my heart that they could have been saved.

One classmate said that she had known one of the shooters since he was in the sixth grade. "He was always angry," she said, "and I never once saw him let his anger out."

A guy this angry isn't going to sign up to go to youth group. We need to try new methods of outreach if we want to make a difference with the kids everybody else has written off.

I believe that if there had been a Rocketown

ministry in Littleton and a counselor like Sean Henegard hanging out at Columbine, this problem could have been avoided. Rocketown is a ministry we started a few years ago that focuses on reaching out to lost teens. We provide an atmosphere loaded with good music and caring counselors.

I'm convinced that Sean Henegard and other Rocketown counselors would have picked Dylan and Eric out. They have an amazing gift that leads them to the most troubled individuals. They also have the patience to wait until a troubled teen is willing to speak on his own terms.

I've seen it happen. I've visited the club and seen some of the most hardened faces you could imagine. Some of the kids look like actors portraying the experience of being lost, hating God, and wanting nothing to do with love. The "fleshly" part of me says, *There is no way that kid can be changed. He just has too much garbage. He's too close-minded to hear what he needs to hear.* And yet, three months later, I'll be back at the club and hear how the guy finally opened up, spilled his heart to a counselor, threw off his hatred and apathy, and gave his heart to the Lord.

The same thing could have happened with Dylan and Eric, if the church had gotten to them in time.

I believe in spiritual warfare. I also believe that the gifts of the Holy Spirit are as valid today as they were two thousand years ago. I believe that people can be demon possessed, and I wouldn't discount the possibility that Eric Harris and Dylan Klebold were possessed. Since I never met them, I have no way of knowing what went wrong or why they stayed up late at night, thinking of ways to kill their classmates. Certainly, demonic influence is one possible explanation, but we'll never know for sure.

Another possible explanation concerns their parents. I was quoted out of context in one interview that said I don't blame the parents. In truth, I don't think we can point our fingers their way and say, "It's all your fault." On the other hand, I certainly believe that Columbine should be a wake-up call to parents across America. I don't understand how kids can make bombs and have firearms lying out in their rooms while their parents remain clueless about what's going on.

In the afterword to Misty Bernall's book, *She Said Yes,* I wrote:

What challenges me most was the willingness of Misty and her husband to make sacrifices in order to rescue Cassie from self-destruction . . .

Cassie's story reminds us that in simple, concrete acts of sacrificial love, a dramatic difference can be made in a young person's life. Through prayer and painstaking effort, Cassie's parents were truly able to help their daughter. Am I ready and willing to put forth such effort with my children? What will my wife and I do if, God forbid, we too are faced with such a drastic situation? At the very least, Misty reminds us of the importance of communicating with our kids, and involving ourselves in our children's lives. It's a matter of making choices. It's not enough just to "be there." As parents, do we know, or even care, what our kids are *really* into? Are we even too scared to know? . . .

Misty's honest portrayal as well as the personal struggles Cassie faced before her death give me hope. We can all change. No child need be lost to self-hate and estrangement. Our choices do matter and they can turn things around, if we are willing to pay the price.[1]

As a parent, I make sure I stay involved—even when my kids don't want me to be! One time I told my son Ryan, "Hey, Ryan, we need to talk about a few things, and sex is one of them," and Ryan responded, "Dad, I don't want to talk about sex."

"That's fine, Ryan," I said, "but we're going to talk about sex anyway!" And we did.

OPENING THE DOOR TO YOUR PARENTS

Some of you reading this book may have parents who don't initiate conversation with you. Maybe you've tried to talk to them, but they showed little or no interest in talking back. It's like they live in their world and you live in yours, and these two worlds never intersect. What do you do then?

First, remind yourself that your parents probably do care. They might not know *how* to show it, but if you went down deep enough, you'd find that most adults want to be good parents. Some of them just don't know how. They are mystified by your world. They feel incompetent, maybe even scared. They just don't know how to talk to you.

Many young people confide in me. One teen told

me about the problems he was having with his dad. I happened to know his father, so I told him, "Your dad really wants to be a good dad. He's trying. He just doesn't know how. At least do your part. It's not your total responsibility—I'm not saying that—but at least try to open up and communicate, for your sake as much as his. Don't get bitter because he closes up; all that does is make you close up, and then you both live in the silence that you hate."

I'm not making empty promises here, but most teens can at least try to open the door with their parents. To do that, some of these phrases work pretty well:

- "Hey, Mom, can we talk?"
- "Hey, Dad, I'm sorry. That didn't come out the way I meant it to."
- "Hey, Mom, what would you do in my situation?"
- "What do you think, Dad?"

Ryan asks me this last question all the time. He wants to know what I think about the movies we watch or the movie scripts he's written. You know what? Sometimes we disagree! After one movie—

which I thought was a total dog—Ryan stood and said, "Absolutely brilliant! The director's a genius."

Initially, I didn't see what Ryan saw, but because I respect him, I was able to listen to him and at least understand where he was coming from. But there are times when I just can't take it. Ryan was all excited about this new music group he had discovered, so he asked me into his room and played the first track. After about a minute I said, "Ryan, my head's going to explode if we don't change the track! I don't get it."

"You don't like that?" Ryan asked, surprised.

"I don't get it," I repeated.

One of the reasons Ryan and I can talk to each other is because Ryan allows me to be honest with him. He knows he isn't always going to like my opinions, and I know he won't always agree with mine. But we keep talking. We keep communicating.

Are you willing to do that with your parents? Are you willing to ask their opinions, even when you know they might disagree with you?

Some of you may have parents with serious problems. After just about every concert, I hear stories from teenagers that break my heart. All I can say is,

"Don't give up on your parents." If your parents aren't Christians, consider yourself a "beachhead" in your home for God—a place where He can break through to the rest of your family. Maybe He can use you to win them to the Lord.

The best thing you can do for your parents is to pray for them. I'm a huge believer in the power of prayer—it turns things around. Instead of griping about how your parents fall short of your ideal, ask yourself, *When was the last time I spent time really praying for my parents, their marriage, and their faith (or lack of faith)?* If you're in your teens, you're not a child anymore. God can use you in powerful ways if you'll let Him. He can even use you to "spiritually parent" your parents by bringing them to Him.

The key is not to hold yourself back because you don't have the best dad or mom, but to realize that you *do* have the best heavenly Father. A good friend of mine was sexually abused by his uncle and all but abandoned by his dad. He had every reason to be screwed up, bitter, and angry. A lot of guys in his situation would have turned out to be the hardened God-haters that sometimes show up at Rocketown.

Instead of losing it, however, this man learned to

let himself be fathered by God. He learned to let God love him and provide him with the security he had never known at home. Through reading Scripture, he came to see how God is always there—even in our darkest moments, even in the times of our deepest shame—and how God had never turned His back. He was always there, just waiting for my friend to turn to Him.

Don't let what you *don't* have close your eyes to what you *can* have: a radical relationship with a God who loves you more than you'll ever know. When I'm one-on-one with kids, I pray that the Holy Spirit will reveal God's desire to father them. Satan has done everything he can to take God's fatherhood away from believers. We've got to fight to get it back. It's our heritage. God really does love you. He really wants to spend time with you, provide for you, and protect you. When you realize that, your life will change.

RADICAL RELATIONSHIP

The next question you have is probably, How can I have this radical relationship with God? From talking to many teens and their parents, I'm very aware that having such a relationship is easy to talk about, but not always so easy to experience.

Sometimes I think we make prayer too difficult. If getting down on your knees and closing your eyes doesn't "do it" for you—if it leads to sleep rather than prayer—that doesn't mean you can't pray. It simply means you need to find a different way to pray.

One of my favorite times to pray is when I take a walk. There's something about walking and being outdoors that keeps my spirit attuned to God's presence. I may not be on my knees, but my soul is still tuned in to God's heart.

Don't get me wrong—there's a place for fully focused, reverent prayer, when you're down on your face before the Holy God of the universe. But other times, we can build our relationship with God by talking to Him just like we'd talk to anyone else.

My most meaningful spiritual experiences rarely take place in a church. Some of my most powerful times of prayer—moments when I was virtually knocked off my feet by the glory of God's presence—occurred when I was in a hospital, watching my wife giving birth. Childbirth is a mess, but it's also a radically holy moment. When you see this tiny, wrinkled face at the top of a white-encrusted body, an umbilical cord still connecting its body to your wife, you realize what a miracle life is. Each time I have watched Deb give birth, I have felt God's presence so much that I was blown away.

I have had other meaningful times of prayer outdoors. Once, when our family was hiking in Beaver Creek, Colorado, we went up a hill we hadn't climbed before and were greeted by the changing aspens. Some were yellow, but others hadn't succumbed to autumn's touch and were still bright green. When we reached the top of the hill, I looked at the beauty of nature and thought, *It looks like God took a paintbrush and colored all this for our pleasure. How can people not believe in God when they see scenes like this?*

My most powerful times of prayer almost always occur when I'm surrounded by nature. C. S. Lewis once said that all churches should be roof-less, for this very reason: worshipers would be over-come by the world God has fashioned, rather than shut up in their man-made boxes.

Learn to open your eyes to the little things, to the tiny glimmers of God's presence. A couple of years ago, I was driving around and passed some Bradford pear trees in full bloom. It's hard to describe what happened next, but it was truly a spiritual experience. Something about the beauty of one of those white trees in full bloom revealed just a glimmer of God's glory, and I lost it. I had to pull over and take it all in. God was so real to me, literally pouring Himself out through the sight of that Bradford tree.

"Quiet times"—those times you spend reading the Bible and praying—are great, but you're missing out on a lot if you think that's the only way to relate to God.

If you *really* want to experience God as Father, though, you'll need to do more than just pray. You'll need to worship. Worship is extremely vital, the lifeblood of our faith. Kids all across the country are tuning in to worship. I've never seen quite as strong a movement of the Holy Spirit among kids as I'm seeing now—eight-, nine-, and ten-year-olds are worshiping God with all their hearts, their arms raised toward heaven.

The reason worship is so important is that *before you can be bold for God, you need to enjoy God.* The students at Columbine were bold because their hearts delighted in God. They couldn't deny Him because they loved Him with all their hearts. If you want to build your boldness, start worshiping.

After worship and prayer, we need to remember the importance of making the right choices.

LITTLE CHOICES, BIG PROBLEMS

"Jim" knew he had a problem. Because he never could stay away from alcohol for very long, he and his wife decided not to have children. Jim was in his late thirties when his medical situation became serious. His liver went bad—that eventually happens to most alcoholics—and he had to have his gall bladder removed. The antibiotics he was given after the operation began destroying the bacteria in his body.

Unfortunately, antibiotics can destroy "good" as well as "bad" bacteria, leaving parts of the body unprotected. When you stop taking the antibiotics, you become vulnerable to bacterial infection. That's what happened to Jim. As a result of the infection, his colon ruptured. He was taken to emergency surgery, but it did no good. Jim was so weak from all that had happened that he died at the way-too-young age of forty-one.

Forty-one may sound old to some of you, but it is only half of a person's normal life expectancy. Jim's premature demise shows the deadly effect of leaning on the wrong crutch.

Jim started drinking heavily when he was sixteen. Though he was just forty-one when he died, he had abused alcohol for twenty-five years, and the alcohol finally claimed its revenge.

What starts out as fun can too often become a habit. A habit can become an addiction, and before you know it, you can be dead or seriously ill, long before your time has come.

Eric Harris and Dylan Klebold probably never imagined themselves as mass murderers. When they were five- and six-year-old kids, they didn't aspire to being called "monsters" by a major news-magazine. So what happened?

They made some very poor "little" choices that eventually led to big problems. Christian radio talk-show host Bob Larson traveled to Littleton just after the shootings. He got kids at Columbine to open up to him and tell him some of the stuff that the media wasn't reporting.

One kid told Bob that both Eric and Dylan got involved in Wicca, a form of witchcraft. Another said they smoked pot and wanted to make a "statement" on April 20, International Pot Day. Others have mentioned how the two killers were influenced by movies, music, video games, and the like.[2] But there isn't just one missing piece of the puzzle that can explain everything away.

Eric and Dylan started by making poor choices. Those choices affected them, shaped them, and led to even worse choices. Ultimately, their choices killed them—and thirteen others.

Because of sin, all of us are born with the capacity to act like monsters. Any one of us could easily self-destruct. Because of the death and resurrection of Jesus Christ, however, all of us are also given the opportunity to repent and start acting like honorable, decent people. None of us can live "good" lives on our own. We need help. We need God. But with His Spirit living in us, we can begin to make wise choices and eventually build a meaningful life.

I've learned to value the importance of "little" choices. It's like putting a record together. You don't start out with a finished product. You start out with a tune, maybe a chorus. You add a few verses, you add the accompaniment, the supporting instruments, and before you know it, you have a song. Then you have to repeat the entire process for ten or eleven more tunes.

Life is like that. Each day we add to our "record," our "book." We choose our friends, we choose what music we listen to, and we decide what we'll think about all day long. Every moment, we're deciding whether we're going to include more of God in our lives or whether we're going to ignore Him. These choices take us down a path. They shape our lives, and eventually we're left with a finished product.

Think about your "little" choices today. Are they taking you down the right path?

HURTING KIDS

Whether your tendency is to view Eric and Dylan

as monsters or as hurting kids, if someone had gotten to them in time, they might have become committed Christians—maybe even tomorrow's Franklin Graham or Frank Peretti.

But we lost Eric and Dylan, as well as twelve other kids who died at their hands. We can do better. As parents, we can become more involved in our kids' lives. By involved, I mean much more than hanging out with them. I mean digging deep, finding out what's bugging them, helping them work through the minefield of adolescence.

Teens from broken or dysfunctional families can still take solace in the fatherhood of God. Learn to love Him. Learn to let Him love you. Get creative in your prayer life, whether that means that you pray with a guitar in your hand, while you're on top of a skateboard, or while swimming laps in a pool. The important thing is to open your heart to God and learn to receive the acceptance and fathering you've always craved.

You know what? All of us can act like monsters. But we can also choose to accept Christ and become saints. The choice is up to us.

CHAPTER 4

RICH RICH

THE COLUMBINE TRAGEDY hit on some sore nerves from my past and helped me come to grips with the early passing of some old friends.

Rich Mullins' music changed my life. To this day, I can say that he has been my favorite artist in our industry. Nobody wrote songs like Rich. He tapped into something incredible when he composed "Creed" and "Hold Me, Jesus" (my favorite Rich Mullins song, other than "Awesome God"). I think that what made Rich unique is that his music doesn't just entertain me; it also ministers to me and deepens my passion for God.

Rich liked to live on the edge. We weren't exactly best friends, but we did know each other well enough to thoroughly enjoy the time we had together. When we saw each other, usually on the road, we hugged each other, and I admired him more every time I spoke with him.

I admired Rich because he was so "out." He lived on the edge and took risks. Part of me envied him, particularly the way he lived on an Indian reservation and shunned the commercial aspects of the music business in his pursuit of living out a pure faith. He didn't have a cell of commercialism in his body; he couldn't care less about the money. All of his possessions would probably have fit in a five-foot-by-five-foot closet. As a married man with kids, I have responsibilities that Rich didn't have (I have no regrets about the life I've chosen), but it was kind of fun to see how Rich handled his life.

One thing marked Rich more than any other: though he was free from the concerns of this world, he was very uncomfortable about the skin he was in. "Restless" was his middle name. I always got the feeling that he wanted to go home to heaven more than hang around in this world, as if he didn't belong here. All of us are just passing through, but Rich always seemed to be looking for the "fast forward" button, moving a few tracks ahead so he could get there a little faster than the rest of us.

In September 1997, I was getting ready to play a concert in Charlotte, North Carolina, when I saw Randy Stonehill walking toward me. He had played earlier in the day, and the look on his face was serious.

"What's going on?" I asked.

"I hate to be the bearer of bad news," he said.

"What's up?"

"Rich Mullins has gone to be with his Father. He's left us."

My mind was preoccupied with getting ready to do a concert for fifteen thousand people. I didn't understand what Randy was trying to tell me. "What are you talking about?" I asked.

"Rich was killed in a car accident last night."

These stark words just about knocked me over. I sat there, stunned, finally muttering a few parting words to Randy: "Thanks for telling me."

But inside, my first thought was, *Why now? Why did Stonehill lay this on me just before I'm supposed to sing to fifteen thousand people? I'm due on stage in fifteen minutes!*

Randy left me in shock. The roar of fifteen thousand eager fans brought me back to reality, but even as I contemplated the set, I remembered that our first song was "Step by Step," a Rich Mullins tune.

The band and I always pray together before a performance, so I called them together and said, "Guys, I've got some bad news. Rich Mullins was killed in a car accident last night. Normally, I would have told you this afterwards, but I just found out about it, and I'm having a really hard time processing it. Pray for me so that I can get through this show. Let's pray for Rich's family, too."

We finished praying just before we had to go on. Immediately, the band and I knew this wasn't just another concert. We were all intensely focused, as if electricity were shooting through the air and charging us up. We were unusually tight, determined to face this struggle together.

I didn't know what would happen or how I would make it past even the first song, especially since Rich had written it. But when I got on stage, my adrenaline literally let loose. In a strange way, Rich's death gave me new life. My music and performance was supercharged. I was so "up," I wondered if I'd explode.

Somewhat surprised by this sudden burst of adrenaline, I just decided to see what would happen. Occasionally, the reality of Rich's death would hit me and almost make me stumble in the middle of a song, but I just told myself, *Don't go there. Don't think about that right now.* Instead, I concentrated on the lyrics of the song or getting the music right.

Some nights you're "on," and some nights you just get through. This was definitely an "on" night. Death had brought amazing life, which is the last thing I thought it would do. I thought this would be our worst show of the year—before the concert, I almost felt sorry for the audience—but it ended up being the opposite. Rich's death absolutely set me ablaze.

By the time we finished the last song, the audience was screaming so loudly that I thought they'd bring the walls down. In fact, I am convinced it was our best performance that year.

I don't know why Rich's death inspired me to do my best work. It sounds like a cliché to say I gave it 125 percent, but that's what I did. I gave the audience literally everything I had, pouring out more emotion, energy, and feeling in my music than perhaps I ever had before.

By the end of the concert, I didn't have an ounce of energy left. I practically limped off the stage, half-dazed, and for the first time I really didn't have the strength to meet with anybody afterwards. Meeting the fans and kids who are hurting has always been an important part of touring for me, but this night, I just didn't have it in me to do that. I was devastated. Because of our duty to perform, I had put aside my feelings about Rich's death. Now my feelings came rushing back, overwhelming me with grief. I didn't even make it to my dressing room before I broke down in tears.

I cried uncontrollably until there couldn't have been a drop of water left in my body. My throat was sore, my eyes stung, and my neck hurt from the tension, but I felt strangely washed inside. Christians weep, but when we cry, the tearstains left behind are marked by healing and hope. I rose tired, but not in despair. It hit me that Rich had all that he wanted. He had always lived with an intense hunger for heaven, and now that hunger was finally satisfied.

Rich was rich—spiritually speaking. He didn't care about earthly wealth, though he made plenty of money from his songs. Even so, he hungered after heavenly riches. That's what he really wanted; that's what motivated him, pushed him to live on the edge, fueled his restless spirit. Finally, that hunger was met. I would miss him, but he was right where he wanted to be.

THE TIDES OF GRIEF

The very next day, I sang at a Franklin Graham concert in the Midwest. I was still reeling over Rich's death; the death of a loved one isn't something you deal with in one good cry. I once heard a Christian counselor—Dr. Kevin Leman—say that experiencing the death of someone you care about is like watching the tides. Sometimes the tide comes in, unusually full and strong. It can catch you unaware, when you least expect it, and almost knock you over. Maybe you hear a song that reminds you of the lost loved one; perhaps you see someone who, at a distance, looks like the person who died. In these instances, you are immediately washed over with sadness, emotionally drowning in the absence of someone you really cared about.

Sometimes the "tide" goes out, leaving you alone for a while. Your pain is still there, but it's much less intense, more of a dull ache than a stinging jolt. You know the hard-core grief will return eventually, but it's holding back for now.

The death of someone you love is never something you "get over." It's something you learn to live with.

After Franklin gave a heartfelt call to embrace the gospel, hundreds of people started streaming toward the front, a sea of seekers, all rushing toward the shore of salvation. He led the crowd in a prayer, and then Franklin ended with his characteristic, "At 8:35 P.M. on September 20, God heard your prayer, and you are a new creature in Christ Jesus."

That was our cue. Tommy Coomes from the Maranatha praise band stood up and said, "We'd like to sing a song that was written by a good friend of ours, Rich Mullins, who has gone to be with the Lord." The band immediately starting playing "Awesome God," and I couldn't help thinking, *Surely Rich hears what's going on down here—and he's pumped!* Tears streamed down my cheeks, but I didn't care. I was happy for my friend, a little sad for me and his family, but overall, thankful for a life lived right. Rich didn't limp into heaven; he charged into it and fell right into his Father's arms.

I CAN'T WAIT TO GET TO HEAVEN

Another "restless" musician I met was Keith Green. A friend and I wrote to him in the mid-seventies and asked him to play at our school. I was just nineteen then, and what a thrill it was for me to pick him up at the airport.

Keith was a quiet man, but he had a passionate underside that came out as soon as he sat down at the piano. He was pretty scruffy—we all were back then—but when his fingers touched the piano keys, his spirit seemed to come alive.

As I watched Keith play and listened to him sing—part sermon, part entertainment—I thought, *That's my dream. If I get lucky, maybe I'll be able to do a record one day.*

As I took him back to the airport, I realized that Keith was a man on a mission. It was almost like he was here to get a job done, and then leave.

The chorus of one of his songs said, "I can't wait to get to heaven." Keith sang these words with all sincerity. Just like Rich, he couldn't wait to get to "the other side."

Ironically, it was just before I cut my first album

when I heard that Keith had died in a plane crash. He had been such a powerful influence on the Christian music industry, inspiring many while also making a few enemies. There wasn't an executive alive who could keep Keith quiet! His prophet's personality certainly pushed the envelope. But death silenced him in a way that no one else could. People still listen to his music, but his sudden passing planted the initial seed in my belief that there is no security in this world. None of us knows how long we'll last.

It was sobering to realize I couldn't count on the future. Every time I cut an album now, I'm keenly aware that it could be my last.

Cassie, Rich, Keith—one died by a violent act, another died in a car, the other died in a plane. All these deaths were unexpected. Their time on earth ended way too soon by my account, but it was perfect timing by God's account. None of us can know when "our time" will come. All we can do is to be ready every day and live with the values of eternity marking our brief time on this earth.

Living through these losses has made me resolve to live each day as if it were my last. I try to make sure I say things I really want to. Fortunately, the last thing Misty Bernall told Cassie was, "Bye, Cass. I love you." And Cassie's last words to Misty were, "Love you too, Mom." We need to remember that we can never be sure we will get a second chance to take back something we've said or to say what we neglected to say.

After Cassie's death, Misty and Brad went through some of her books. In one book, *Discipleship: Living for Christ in the Daily Grind,* Cassie had underlined these words:

All of us should live life so as to be able to face eternity at any time.[1]

When she underlined this sentence, she had no idea how prophetic these words were.

CHAPTER 5

MINI-MARTYRDOMS

MOST OF US will never have a gun pointed to our head, as did Cassie. However, there are other life events that represent "our time"—moments when our faith will be truly tested.

Hollywood erupted into a furor early in 1999 when the board of the Motion Picture Academy of Arts and Sciences announced that Elia Kazan, director of legendary films such as *A Streetcar Named Desire, East of Eden,* and *On the Waterfront,* would receive an honorary Oscar for lifetime achievement during the spring Academy Awards ceremony. Nobody debated whether Kazan's work was worthy of such recognition. The controversy came from a choice Elia made back in 1952. For several years prior, the House Un-American Activities Committee (HUAC) had interrogated Hollywood insiders—directors, producers, actors, and screenwriters—in an attempt to uncover a Communist conspiracy.

Kazan had been a member of the Communist

party, but he left it when Communist party leaders started trying to dictate how he should make his pictures favorable to a socialist agenda. During an appearance before HUAC, Kazan confirmed a list of Hollywood insiders who had also been members. It was a tough, gut-wrenching decision for him to make. In his autobiography, Kazan wrote, "A difficult decision means either way you go, you lose."[1]

On the side of testifying was whether the secrecy surrounding membership in the Communist party should be broken for the sake of democracy and national security. At that time, the Communist party made no secret of its ultimate aim to overturn the U.S. government and replace it with a socialist one. HUAC traditionally appealed to witnesses' patriotism when it asked them to talk.

On the negative side, Kazan knew that many of those so named would be blacklisted. In fact, a number of their careers suffered irreparable harm when it was revealed that they were communist sympathizers (Kazan never provided the committee with any new information, however; he simply confirmed names they already had in their possession).

What would you do? What principles would guide

you through a choice between the security and free-dom of your country (including that of your family and friends) and your colleagues' right to privacy?

These are the moments that are much more common in today's society, times when our faith will be tested every bit as much as if somebody had a gun pointed to our head. For instance, what if, during a summer job, you worked at an appliance store. A customer returned a refrigerator because it was scratched. Your boss had the scratch painted, then told you to deliver the appliance and tell the customer it was a brand-new one.

Would you lie to keep your job?

This is a real-life scenario, by the way. The Christian who faced it handled it brilliantly, in my opinion. He looked his boss in the eye and said, "I will never lie *to* you, nor will I ever lie *for* you."

I heard about a woman who aspired to become a novelist. She worked long and hard, suffered and endured many rejections, until finally a publisher offered her a contract for her book. There was just one problem.

"For us to make this book commercially viable," the publisher explained, "we need you to include at least two explicit sex scenes, three to five pages each. If you'll add these, we'll publish the book."

This woman walked away from a lifelong dream rather than compromise on her principles.

I've also heard of actresses who finally got their break—until they learned that the director was insisting on nudity. "I can do this without explicit nudity," one actress tried to argue, but the director wouldn't budge. At that moment, she had to choose between the part of a lifetime or remaining true to her conscience.

The gun pointed at Cassie's head was literal. Our guns will usually be figurative. When that time comes, will we be as strong as Cassie? How can we get to the place where we'll lay down our lives instead of compromising during the time of testing? I can think of three responses to those questions:

- We need to become leaders instead of followers.
- We need to focus our desires onto another world.
- We need to learn the art of self-denial.

Let's look at each of these in turn.

A LEGACY OF LEADERSHIP

A century ago, Sonia Keppel believed her mother had a "brilliant, goddesslike quality," in part because of the expensive flowers and gifts sent to her by King Edward VII. Sonia's eyes filled with the orchids and "beribboned baskets" delivered in horse-drawn vans by a coachman decked out in the king's finest. At the time, Mrs. Keppel's affair with the king did not destroy her marriage or her reputation—but times have changed. Sonia's granddaughter (and Mrs. Keppel's great-granddaughter) grew up to be Camilla Parker Bowles, long-standing mistress of Charles, the Prince of Wales and somewhat tragic husband of Lady Diana Spencer.

Whether we intend to or not, all of us are leaving behind some kind of legacy. This legacy will either inspire others around us—including our children—to live for the Lord, or it will pass on a message that may negatively effect several generations after us.

I encourage you to leave behind a legacy of leadership. I've got a real simple definition for a leader and a follower: A leader is someone who stands up for what he or she believes in; a follower is someone who compromises. We need more leaders, people who are secure in their beliefs and who are willing (and determined) to bring the crowd to their side rather than follow after the weakness of everybody else.

Anytime you find yourself compromising your beliefs, you have become a follower. Obviously, you're not too secure about what you believe in the first place—at least, not secure enough to be laughed at for it or to face the spite of a disbelieving world. Or maybe you don't really believe what you've been saying. Maybe you *think* the gospel is true, but you're not *sure,* so you're willing to follow God only when it's convenient.

There's something funny about the gospel: The more you suffer for it, the more you believe in it. The first time you stand up to opposition, you feel ten feet tall. Nobody can knock you down. You're more convinced than ever of the gospel's truth.

In the same way, the more you compromise, the less you believe in God. When you act out of doubt, you only *increase* your doubt and put yourself on a dangerous, downward slide. That's because *what we do affects how we believe.* There's no getting around this.

Obedience breeds obedience, just as disobedience leads to more disobedience. When you stand up boldly, you walk away saying to yourself, *They're laughing, but I did the right thing.* The sense of faith that overwhelms you is so strong that the next time you're in a similar situation, you won't have to think twice about standing up for God. It gets even easier the third and fourth time, until you don't know any other way.

In a negative way, the same thing happens when we compromise. People who cut corners keep lowering the bar of their faith, accepting greater and greater compromise in their lives. They may not be aware of it at first, but someday they'll wake up and wonder how they got so far away from God's will and plan for their lives. Their faith will be a distant memory. (I sing about this in my song "Missing Person.")

We usually don't "fall away" with one giant leap, but rather with consistent baby steps.

Every day, we have two choices: We can leave behind a legacy of hypocrisy, or we can leave a legacy of leadership. A legacy is something that develops over time. It is not built in a day, a month, or even a year. A legacy may be built in a decade, but it can also be destroyed with one act of compromise.

I challenge you to leave behind a legacy of leadership. Let people know you stand for something, that your faith in God is part of who you are, and that it's something you'll never give up on or compromise for.

In the end, people will respect you more for leaving a legacy they disagree with than for straddling the fence or deciding to go with the crowd.

I've been singing about my faith for eighteen years. I really believe what I'm talking about, and I'm unshakable in it. I want to leave behind a legacy of uncompromised faith. To do that, I have to watch myself. I've seen how others have fallen, and it's kept me on my toes. One story that really affected me, in part because the man wanted to reach out to kids like I do, is the story of Paul Reubens.

A TARNISHED LEGACY

In 1980, a young comedian named Paul Reubens felt like his big chance had come and gone. He finally got an audition for *Saturday Night Live,* the show that has launched more comedic careers than any other production, but was beat out by Gilbert Gottfried. For a moment, Reubens wondered if he would ever get another chance.

Have you ever been in a place like this, just after a dream has been squashed, and you wonder if you can go on?

Ironically, his *SNL* rejection proved to be essential to Reubens's eventual success. *SNL* collapsed into one of its least funny seasons ever while Reubens struck it rich with his own comedic stage production called *The Pee-wee Herman Show.*

Reubens's show played for five months and led to a sleeper hit film, *Pee-wee's Big Adventure,* which in turn helped launch a hugely successful Saturday morning television show called *Pee-wee's Playhouse.* Before its run was over, *Pee-wee's Playhouse* garnered twenty-two Emmys.

Success was costly, however. Reubens burned himself out with demanding roles as writer, producer, star, and virtual codirector. When Reubens quit making the show in 1990, he was, in his words, "an empty shell."

In the summer of 1991, Reubens visited his parents in Sarasota, Florida. He had plans to visit some friends for dinner, but to kill time until then, he stopped off at an X-rated theater.

The next sixty minutes destroyed all that Reubens had accomplished during the previous sixty months.

As Reubens left the theater, he was arrested by Sarasota policemen and charged with indecent exposure and another offense. Since he was out of costume, the police officers didn't immediately realize he was Pee-wee Herman, but two days later a reporter recognized Reubens's name while skimming through police reports. The journalist tipped off the press, and Paul's life caved in.

After the arrest, *People* magazine named Reubens one of the "25 most intriguing people of 1991." For years Paul had worked hard to make kids laugh—and he was good at it—but never did *People* see fit to honor him for this work. No, it wasn't until he really blew it in an extremely embarrassing situation that *People* found him "intriguing." Paul had to come to grips with the fact that suddenly, he wasn't known for his work as a writer, actor, or director. He was now notorious for frequenting theaters that show porn.

Reubens told an interviewer how sick this made

him feel. "I thought . . . the amount of time and energy and work that I put into entertaining kids, fighting the good fight, and I've become an intriguing person for *this?*"[2]

Pee-wee had gained quite a bit of fame that went along with his twenty-two Emmys—but nothing like the notoriety that blanketed Reubens after his arrest.

Just one act of compromise can destroy a legacy of leadership. We need to be careful. God is forgiving, but the world can be pretty cruel when they see us compromise.

Beyond aspiring to leave a consistent legacy of leadership, we need to focus our affections on another world.

A SATISFYING WORLD

There are parts of this world and moments in this life that are very, very good, very satisfying, soul stirring, life-giving. Sometimes when you're on stage, the adrenaline is incredible. You feel like you can't contain the energy that's flowing between you and the audience. It's like a natural high, and you start to fear that if it doesn't fade, you'll literally explode from the energy that's pouring out. You'd pass out if it didn't end; that's how incredible it is.

Athletes might be able to relate to this. I felt a little like this when my high school football team won the state championship. People started going crazy. In some weird way, you touch transcendence. The struggle, the hurts and bruises from a hard-hitting contest—all fade away in the thrill of ending the season on top.

I've even felt this vicariously when watching my kids' games. I'm a huge football fan anyway, but watching my kids' high school team, when I know most of the boys and have watched them get beat to a pulp more than once, there was something special about a particular come-from-behind victory. Their team was down 12 to 7 late in the fourth quarter, with the ball on their own eight-yard line. They drove the ball down to their opponent's fourteen-yard line with eight seconds to go.

The quarterback dropped back, found his man in the end zone, and connected for the win.

I went berserk.

I've experienced other highlights, including playing at Camp David and the White House. I'm not sure why George and Barbara Bush kept inviting us to play for them, but it has always been a blessing. We were up at Kennebunkport once, and the president smiled as he said to me, "Well, Michael, you gotta sing for your supper."

I sat down at an old upright piano—about half of the keys were in tune—and worked my way through a few songs. When I launched into "Friends," I looked up and saw Barbara Bush's eyes tear up.

That will always be a highlight in my life, no doubt about it. But you know what? I couldn't care less about schmoozing with powerful people. I loved being with the Bushes because of who they are, not because George was president at the time. By itself, playing at the White House doesn't particularly appeal to me, except for the fact that I believe there is an eternal purpose and reason for why I have led worship with senators and those in the White House.

This eternal reason is why I'd be willing to leave this world—with all its fun, with all it has to offer, with all the good times left ahead—if my faith required it. There's an even better world than this one that's waiting for me, and I can't wait to get there. As good as parts of this world are, it can't compare to what God is getting ready for us.

Think of what Cassie and Rachel willingly gave up—high school graduation, college, a life on their own, having a family, making their mark on this world . . . They let go of all that in order to testify about their Lord.

No one has ever held a gun to my head. In fact, I've never even been seriously challenged to stand up for my faith. Sure, in junior high I made some tough decisions, but nothing like Cassie's. In my case, my closest friends started going to all the parties. I knew there was nothing for me there, but my friends wanted me to be a part of that scene simply because they were. Deep inside I knew that if I didn't join them at the parties, there was going to be a change in our friendship, and there was.

Monday-morning conversations were always about the weekend. I could literally feel my friends pulling away, because I couldn't talk with them about the parties. They were "nice" to me, but the "hang thing" was over. I didn't belong anymore.

That was hard. It was no fun to be excluded, but I found my meaning in the Lord. Being excluded day after day gets real old, real fast, but this "mini-martyrdom" was something I was willing to endure because I had found something that mattered even more than popularity: faith in Jesus Christ.

Most of us will never be tested to the extent that Cassie was, but virtually all of us are tested on a regular basis in many smaller ways. Do you ever find yourself pretending you're not a Christian, because you know that what you're doing goes totally against your faith? Do you find yourself holding back from sharing the gospel because you don't want to be laughed at or rejected? Do you compromise on what movies you watch or what music you listen to just so that you can fit in and have something to talk about on Monday morning?

These are the mini-martyrdoms that Christ referred to when he said we must take up our cross *daily* (Luke 9:23). Every compromise is rooted in the fact that we're trying to find our meaning and acceptance in this world instead of the next world, and that's a recipe for leaving behind a legacy of hypocrisy instead of one of leadership.

It's not possible for us to literally die every day, so we know Jesus was referring to spiritual matters when He told us to take up our cross. There's no way we can apply this tough teaching to our lives if we live with the wrong set of priorities.

There's a powerful passage in the Gospel of Matthew. Jesus told the disciples of His impending martyrdom, and Peter didn't like what he heard, so he pulled Jesus aside and said, "Far be it from You, Lord; this shall not happen to You!"

Jesus' response was unbelievably strong: "Get behind Me, Satan! You are an offense to Me, for you are not mindful of the things of God, but the things of men" (Matt. 16:22–23 NKJV).

Peter got off track because his mind was set on this world. Living from that perspective, it didn't make any sense for Jesus to die. If all Cassie lived for was this world, there's no way she would have had the courage to say yes, knowing she might never speak another word. Cassie made a tremendous investment. She gave all, but received even more in return. She is happier today than the richest, most famous person on this earth. She enjoys a closer intimacy with God than the person who spends hours praying. She is worshiping God more perfectly than the most talented musician. Cassie is in a great place because she was willing to turn her back on a good place. Behind every act of compromise is a Christian who is living for this world rather than the next.

The third step to becoming a solid witness for Christ is learning the art of self-denial.

SPIRITUAL DEATHS

Jesus gave His disciples two commands in Luke 9:23: Deny yourself, and take up your cross daily. Without self-denial, we'll shun the cross every time.

Self-denial isn't easy. Maybe you've held a grudge for a long time. Perhaps the grudge is a result of something someone did, deliberately, to hurt you. Even though that person was wrong, you know God wants you to give up the grudge. That's the last thing you want to do. But God is calling you to do it.

Will you obey?

Maybe you're in a relationship, or you're contemplating a relationship, that you know is wrong.

You've been lonely, and you're scared to death of letting this person go. That person seems to meet all your needs, but you know, deep down, the relationship isn't right. You'd rather cut off your right arm than end this relationship. Even the *thought* of losing it hurts so much that it brings you to tears. It would be a "living death" to let it go.

But you know God wants you to. Will you?

The heart of self-denial is trust. God knows what's best for us, and He leads us to the best places and the best relationships . . . as long as we let Him lead. This is the thought behind David's famous Psalm:

> The LORD is my shepherd;
> I shall not want.
> He makes me to lie down in green pastures;
> He leads me beside the still waters.
> He restores my soul. (Ps. 23:1-3 NKJV)

God wants to take you to a good place, but the road may not always appear so friendly. David admitted, "Yea, though I walk through the valley of the shadow of death . . ." In order for David to go to God's promised land, he had to walk the path of death and denial. He had to say no to the shortcuts and shallow resorts along the way that promised fulfillment but would never be able to really deliver.

After David went through the valley of death, he told us:

My cup runs over.
Surely goodness and mercy shall follow me
All the days of my life;
And I will dwell in the house of the LORD
Forever. (vv. 5–6 NKJV)

Will you trust God to take you to this rich place, full of life and meaning and purpose and joy, even though you may not be able to see it right now? Will you let Him lead you through dark places, knowing that His pasture is just ahead, even if you're afraid you might die in that valley? Remember, God won't leave you. David said that God was with him every step of the way. That's the only reason he didn't fear; he said of God, "You are with me; / Your rod and Your staff, they comfort me."

So often, we become Christians hoping and expecting to be blessed. God certainly does His share of blessing, but He also asks us to give up all in return. Life for a Christian is a daily dose of self-denial, but this is a mini-death that leads to new life.

What is the mini-martyrdom God is calling you to today?

HOMESICK

Whether we are willing to take up our cross daily is determined by what we're living for. Part of me is as restless as Rich Mullins was. Sometimes I ache to be with my heavenly Father. The main thing that keeps me here is my family. I want to see what my kids become; I want to hold my grand-children. But if it weren't for that, I'd welcome the thought of an early trip to heaven.

Whenever I return to my hometown in Kenova, West Virginia, I'm reminded of how short life is. Because Kenova is so small, it's easier to keep track of what has happened to everybody. One person who was paralyzed is now dead. The woman who served as my mom's catering partner for years got cancer. Before we knew it, she was gone. And then I see the people who are still living. They were grown-ups when I lived there, and now they look *really* old, and I realize that heaven isn't as far away as I used to think it was. Am I ready to go there?

I believe that Cassie and Rachel were willing to stand up in their moment of testing because they knew that heaven was their real home. If you truly are a committed believer, you have this yearning inside you to go home. You realize that no matter how rich this world can be, it still can't satisfy. You can have all your dreams come true, and yet you still long for more. C.S. Lewis wrote, "If I find in myself desires which nothing in this world can satisfy, the only logical explanation is that I was made for another world."

Our hearts are made for heaven. Nothing short of that will satisfy us. In fact, I believe that, apart from family, ministry in God's kingdom is the only thing that makes this life meaningful. Homesickness afflicts all of God's children.

While most of us will never face a literal life-or-death decision to stand up for God, all of us face spiritual life-or-death choices almost daily. Cassie's courageous response—the simple word *yes*—challenges each of us to face these mini-martyrdoms with a new sense of purpose and obedience.

CHAPTER 6

FRIENDLY FIRE

I WAS SITTING by myself in a Mexican restaurant when one of the most bizarre and tragic news stories of 1999 broke onto the air. A Lear jet was veering wildly off its flight plan. A military chase plane went up to find out what was going on and was reporting that the Lear jet's windows were frosted over—not a good sign, to say the least.

But that's not what caught my attention. My friend, PGA golfer Payne Stewart, was on board. Tragically, Payne and five others died on that flight, which eventually crashed.

I had first met Payne a couple of years before. He came to our Christmas show with his daughter and introduced himself. I liked him from the start and admired the way he was now so up-front about his faith, wearing a WWJD? (What Would Jesus Do?) bracelet as he played. Several times we had planned to play golf together, but our schedules never matched.

I got home late that night and found Deb on the

phone with J. B. Collingsworth, Payne's pastor and a close friend of the Stewart family. I actually know J. B. pretty well myself.

Deb handed the phone over, and I said into the receiver, "This is unbelievable."

J. B. and I talked for a while, and near the end he finally told me why he called. "Michael, Payne's kids told me they really want you to sing at the funeral."

"I'd love to do it, J. B.," I said, "but I'm supposed to be in Calgary on Thursday and Michigan on Friday, so I couldn't get there until Saturday—and you can't do the funeral around me."

"We'll see," he said.

The next day, J. B. called back and said the funeral was scheduled for Friday.

"I just don't think I can make it down there on that day," I said, but then I thought of his kids asking J. B. if I could come and sing "Friends." How could I say no? They had just lost their dad.

"The only way I could pull it off is if I flew all night," I said, very disappointed but considering the matter closed. When I got off the phone, my words came back to haunt me. What if I *did* fly all night?

Wouldn't that make it possible for me to attend? The more I prayed about it, the more I realized that was what I was supposed to do.

Still, it seemed crazy. Calgary is in Alberta, Canada, over 150 miles north of Montana. Payne's funeral was going to be held in Orlando, Florida. I'd have to fly down through Canada and the entire United States to get there. And then I'd have to make it back up to Michigan—back at the top of the U.S.—by Friday afternoon.

It seemed absolutely crazy, in fact, just crazy enough for me to believe that it might be God's will. I called J. B. back and said, "I think I've lost my mind agreeing to do this, but I also think it's what God wants me to do."

We flew up to Calgary, where I played at a Franklin Graham crusade. Franklin was so supportive; as soon I was done he said, "You've got to go." I literally walked off the stage and went directly to my plane. We flew all night, landing in Nashville at about 2:00 A.M. We refueled the plane and took off at 3:00, landing in Orlando at about 5:00 A.M. I went to a hotel and got one hour of sleep, then woke up in time to make it to the church.

I met with Payne's family—his wife, Tracey, and his children, Chelsea and Aaron—just before the funeral. I was impressed by the commitment of First Baptist Church, Orlando. People had gathered in rooms all around the church with one purpose: to intercede for the service, which was being broadcast internationally.

The prayers showed. It was an awesome service. Virtually the entire PGA Tour had flown down to attend and pay their last respects to Payne. PGA officials had interrupted the weekend's event, scheduling twenty-seven holes on Thursday and twenty-seven on Saturday while suspending play on Friday, so that all the professionals could be there. Tiger Woods, Jack Nicklaus, all the biggest names in professional golf, came down.

Even more impressive, millions of people watched the service all over the world, especially in golf and country clubs. J. B. Collingsworth and professional golfer Paul Azinger gave one of the clearest presentations of the gospel I've ever heard. It was amazing, unbelievable. First Baptist of Orlando received calls for weeks after the funeral from people who gave their hearts to the Lord while watching Payne's memorial.

When it came time for me to sing, I got up and started with "Friends." I then went into a slightly revised version of "This Is Your Time," changing the "she" pronouns to "he" to make it fit Payne.

I was blown away as I looked out at the crowd and the television cameras. The song hadn't even been released on an album yet, but here God was using it to reach out to some of the world's most influential people. I couldn't help thinking about Payne what I had thought about Cassie: what Satan intended for harm, God turned around and used for good. Losing Payne was terrible, and we will miss him tremendously, but in giving up his life, the message of salvation reached out to many lost hearts.

A few weeks after the service, I called Tracey, Payne's widow. One of the great tragedies of this plane crash was that there was virtually nothing left of the survivors. Almost everything on board disintegrated. However, Tracey told me that the crash investigators were able to recover three of Payne's belongings—his wedding ring, his SMU ring, and his WWJD? bracelet—all intact. Payne Stewart died with his affection for his wife and family and his commitment to his Lord wrapped around his finger and wrist.

FOR SUCH A TIME

While I sang in front of the world, I kept thinking, *Wow, does God have a plan or what? His ways are higher than our ways.*

With CNN and ESPN carrying this live, I just couldn't believe I was up there. And I couldn't believe how clearly the gospel was being proclaimed on the airwaves around the world.

I remembered my earlier hesitation about writing "This Is Your Time" in the first place. Remember that? I was concerned that people thought I'd be cashing in on a tragedy.

I'm so glad I didn't let that concern win out. I had no idea how this song could minister to people, and I was reminded of the importance of standing up, having a thick skin, and doing what you know God is calling you to do, even though others might question what you're doing.

We've got to be prepared to face the "friendly fire."

A THORN IN KENTUCKY ROSE

"Michael, we've got a problem with the single."

I was on my way to our vacation home in Beaver Creek, Colorado, just after *The First Decade* album was released. This record is a collection of previous top hits with two new singles, "Kentucky Rose" and "Do You Dream of Me?"

Jennifer Cook, the vice president of artist development at Blanton/Harrell, called to let me know of a little problem with "Kentucky Rose."

To give you some background, the song is completely fictitious. It wasn't based on any person in particular, nor is the story it tells something that actually happened. As I wrote the music, I knew the words "Kentucky Rose" had to be in there, but I gave Wayne Kirkpatrick all the freedom he wanted to go from there.

Wayne wrote a great lyric; I was thrilled with what he had done. We created a well-respected preacher and farmer who lived in a tiny town in the foothills of Kentucky.

There he stood—a hearty smile;
You could hear his voice ringing out for a country mile,

And he could place your mind at ease
With his tenderness and a heart
That aimed to please.
A pauper's hands, a farmer's clothes—
Just a preacher man we called Kentucky Rose.

In many ways he was an ideal character—one who embodies the simplicity of faith and the inspiration of a quiet life that is well-lived.

He worked the soul like he worked the land;
He spoke in ways that anyone could understand—
Simple words of simple faith,
And when it came to love
He would go out of his way—
A helping hand,
A soothing chat.
And he practiced what he preached—imagine that!
And, as far as kindness goes,
There was none compared to old Kentucky Rose.

After painting a picture of such a godly man, we put him in a tough situation. He was out for an evening stroll when he saw a boy trapped underneath a bridge, in danger of drowning. Without thinking about his own safety, the farmer/preacher dived into the water and saved the boy's life—but lost his own.

For on that ridge of stone and ice
Kentucky met his Maker in a sacrifice.

What would a country town do when such a man died in such a heroic manner? We thought people would come from miles to celebrate his life.

So peaceful in his Sunday best,
He was buried on a hill and laid to rest;
When people heard, they came in droves
To say their last good-byes to sweet Kentucky Rose.

I couldn't imagine how anyone could find a "problem" in a song like this, which ends with a poetic touch:

Now, on that hill
One flower grows;
They say it is the spirit of Kentucky Rose.[1]

"What's up?" I asked Jennifer.
"I'm holding a fax that is being sent to Christian radio stations all across the country, accusing you of going New Age."

"What? You've got to be kidding me!" It took everything I had not to drive the car off the road.

"Be careful!" Deb said from the passenger seat.

"How could someone say that?" I asked Jennifer.

"He has a problem with the line, *One flower grows/They say it is the spirit of Kentucky Rose*. I guess he's faxing this warning—'There's a thorn in Kentucky Rose'—to every station he can get ahold of, implying that this is some hidden, New Age message."

"This is unbelievable," I replied.

What a way to begin a vacation! Wayne and I had set out to write a song that would inspire people to live their lives with integrity, courage, and faithfulness. Because of one poetic touch, which some man took literally, we were being accused of going New Age! There are hundreds of lines on that album, yet someone who didn't even know me, who didn't even have the courtesy to call me and talk about it, was questioning my faith by taking one line out of context and putting a meaning on it that neither Wayne nor I ever intended.

In all honesty, I was furious. I was angry that someone would question my faith and what I believe in. I couldn't believe that someone who didn't even know me would imply that I'd try to sneak New Age philosophy into my music. He was essentially questioning a reputation I had spent my lifetime trying to build.

When I get in situations like this, I know I need to talk to my pastor. I called Scotty Smith and told him what had happened. He could hear the anger in my voice and tried to help me cool down. At first, Scotty thought of responding himself, but decided to hold off.

"Let's wait a bit before we respond," he said. "Let's let the steam wear off."

I knew Scotty was right, so I tried my best to forget about it. A couple of days later, I realized that it wasn't worth my time to respond. A guy like that probably wouldn't listen anyway. I never did talk to him.

As much as I hate to admit it, his smear campaign probably did have an effect. "Kentucky Rose" is the least successful song I've had on Christian radio. I'm sure this guy had something to do with that. If a song doesn't get played, it doesn't get requested, and it only takes a rumor to get some station managers nervous.

But looking back over my entire career, I really haven't had much criticism from fellow believers. "Place in This World" became a mainstream hit *after* Amy Grant's "Baby, Baby," so I didn't get nearly as much flak from Christians as she did. In fact, I got far more positive response than negative. Moms and dads came up to me after concerts, thanking me for going mainstream and giving their kids something positive to listen to. Only a very small minority of people accused me of selling out. (I still maintain that "Place in This World" is one of the most spiritual songs I've ever recorded, even though it was a Top-40 pop hit.) My response to these people has always been *not* to respond. I don't have anything to say to them, because I don't believe I've done anything wrong. They'll never change my mind, and I doubt I'll ever change theirs, so it's an argument I refuse to get into.

I learned this strategy from Jesus, who was also silent before His religious persecutors. Not that I'm sinless like He was, but Jesus was silent for one compelling reason: He had nothing to defend! And neither, in this instance at least, did I.

EXPECT RESISTANCE

I like to warn kids who are trying to break in to what I call "strategic ministries"—Christians eager to make it in the "secular" world of music, movies, television, business, and news reporting—that their worst attacks may well come from Christians. It's a sad reality, but still true. A committed believer needs to be prepared for attacks from the "world," but an *active* and *creative* believer needs to be prepared for attacks from the Church. If a Christian had to have the unanimous consent and approval from all other Christian churches before stepping out, nothing would ever get done. Even Billy Graham has faced regular attacks throughout his career.

In fact, people have written entire books attacking Billy. Some have created their own personal crusades, trying to get churches to oppose our country's most successful evangelist. Even so, there is probably no more respected religious leader in the history of America.

The Romans weren't Jesus' most vicious critics. In fact, Pilate told the crowd, "You have brought this Man to me, as one who misleads the people.

And indeed, having examined Him in your presence, *I have found no fault in this Man* concerning those things of which you accuse Him; no, neither did Herod, for I sent you back to him; and indeed nothing deserving of death has been done by Him" (Luke 23:14–15, italics added NKJV).

In the eyes of the secular authorities, Jesus was an innocent man. But the *religious authorities* insisted that Jesus be killed. The very group that should have supported the Messiah's ministry instead chose to viciously attack it. It has always been this way and probably always will be.

If God is calling you to do something, go for it! Don't let fear hold you back. The satisfaction that comes from being used by God is far more fulfilling than the sense of being drained from attacks against you.

GOD'S WORK

A few weeks before "This Is Your Time" came out, I got a call from one of the songwriters on the record. He had received the video for "This Is Your Time" in the mail and played it for a non-Christian friend who happened to be with him at the time. That friend started crying and dropped to his knees, giving his heart to the Lord.

There's nothing more exciting than seeing God use you to help someone embrace His message of salvation. Take the risks; it's worth it. One act of obedience to God in the face of human opposition can reap amazing rewards.

Because of Payne Stewart's memorial service, "This Is Your Time" reached millions of people and encouraged numerous grieving souls, even before it was released. God blessed it with a huge number of sales in the first week. My managers were astonished at how many copies sold—featuring a title song I almost didn't want to write!

Don't let fear hold you back. Face the "friendly fire," and watch God lead you into ministry you've only dreamed about.

CHAPTER 7

IF NECESSARY, USE WORDS

CASSIE PREACHED ONE of the most powerful sermons of this century. It was also undoubtedly the shortest: "Yes."

I'm a huge fan of a St. Francis of Assisi quote:

Preach often, and if necessary, use words.

By laying down her life, Cassie put flesh to St. Francis's words. She challenged all of us to a higher level of faith and commitment.

I don't by any means consider myself an expert on Cassie's life, but one thing seems clear. She wasn't an "in your face" Christian. When she asked Jesus into her heart, her friends and family immediately realized that something major had happened to her, but even then she wasn't over the top. When she got back from the retreat where she became a Christian, all Cassie told Misty was, "Mom, I've changed. I've totally changed. I know you are not going to believe it, but I'll prove it to you."

Brad, Cassie's father, noticed the change almost

immediately. It wasn't Cassie's words that convinced him, however. It was her demeanor. "When she left she had still been this gloomy, head-down, say-nothing girl," he said. "But . . . the day she came back she was bouncy and excited about what had happened to her."[1]

Cassie *lived* a sermon of salvation in front of her parents. Misty admits that at first she was very skeptical. Cassie had been so hateful and so rebellious that Misty's hesitation was understandable. But listen to how Misty describes Cassie's reaction to that retreat:

> She didn't get out of that car saying that she'd been saved or anything like that. She wasn't at all emotional. She was very down to earth, very matter of fact: 'Mom, I've changed.' And it really seemed to be true. From then on, Cassie became a totally different person. She never talked much about that weekend, and we never pressed her. But her eyes were bright, she smiled again like she hadn't for years, and she began to treat us (and her brother) with genuine respect and affection.[2]

Cassie wanted to switch from private school to public school so that she could live out her new-found faith in front of other kids her age. She told Misty, "Mom, I can't witness to the kids at Christian school. I could reach out to many more people if I were in a public one."[3]

But even though this was Cassie's aim (her parents finally gave in and enrolled Cassie at Columbine), after Cassie's death, several friends mentioned that Cassie wasn't at all "pushy" in her witness. She didn't use a lot of words. She certainly didn't argue. She just quietly lived out her faith.

SUSPICION

When "Place in This World" became a mainstream Top-40 hit, I was suddenly cast into the world of mainstream executives who ran mainstream stations and record stores—and who often used vulgar language. The world of mainstream music was very intense, and there was awkwardness at first between me and the mainstream executives. These people were suspicious of my faith. They had heard more than their share of sermons from well-meaning Christians about how they were evil and on the highway to hell. The message they had heard was all law, law, law, surrounded by intense accusations.

Naturally, these executives thought I'd be like that. After all, I was a "Christian" singer. I'm sure they were thinking, *Oh, great, we have to work with this blankety-blank gospel singer who plays at Billy Graham crusades and wants to save our souls!*

But I won them over—not with words, but with actions. They came to one of my concerts and were impressed by what they saw. It wasn't at all what they expected. They thought they were coming to an old-time gospel concert, but our show was focused on pop. It was professional, the music was high quality, and there wasn't any heavy sermonizing, but there was a spirit in the arena unlike anything they had heard before.

This might bother some people, but I realize that when I'm on stage, though people are being ministered to, I'm also an entertainer. My "ministry" goes far beyond the stage, such as driving my kids to school, dating my wife once a week, and talking to the guy at the grocery store. That's different from my *vocation*, which is making records. I want people to like the music. I want them to enjoy themselves when they come to a show. Yeah, because of who I am and what I believe in, the music has a "positive" message and people tell me God has really used it in their lives—but I'm also doing my best to put on a really good show.

This approach opened doors with the executives. They found out that I could have a conversation with them without judging them. When they let the expletives fly, I didn't wince and look like they had committed the unpardonable sin. I tried to act like I saw Jesus act in the film that depicts the Gospel of Matthew. Jesus entered the tax collector's house where the tax collectors and other sinners were partying it up. He didn't rail against them or let fly with heat-seeking verbal missiles. Instead, Jesus started telling stories. He quietly won them over.

This is the same approach that Peter recommended for Christians who are married to unbelievers. Though he was talking to the women, the principle is the same for men. Peter said that wives should live in such a way that unbelieving husbands "may be won over without words by the behavior of their wives, when they see the purity and reverence of your lives" (1 Peter 3:1–2 NIV).

You could use this same verse for Christians who have non-Christian parents, roommates, in-laws, you name it. Before you tell these people how the gospel can change them, let them see how it has already changed you. Once people *see* the gospel in our lives they'll be far more willing to *hear* the gospel from our lips.

I know a woman who remained true to her God throughout a heartbreaking divorce. Her husband insisted on breaking up the marriage. Instead of growing bitter, this woman drew closer to God. She drew serenity and peace from her Lord and used the time apart from her husband to grow in Christlikeness. She held out hope for her marriage to get back together until the day her ex-husband remarried. She then quietly removed her ring and started on her new life as a single woman.

Shortly thereafter, she got a call from her father. "I've watched what you've gone through," he said. "I've seen how you've reacted, and I want what you have." This woman had the great privilege of leading her sixty-two-year-old father to the Lord.

That's exactly what I'm talking about: staying faithful in our actions so that people eventually come to us asking why we behave the way we do. Then they'll really listen to our words.

IN THE WORLD

If we're never around nonbelievers, we'll never be able to show them a different way of life. I'm not suggesting that all of us should start hanging out at bars, but I *am* suggesting that we be careful about creating Christian country clubs. If you were to ask Harrison Ford or Fiona Apple to list the top five contemporary Christian musicians or groups, you'd probably be met with a blank stare. They don't have a clue. The fault isn't with the Hollywood crowd as much as it is with those of us who have created a separate world that never intersects with theirs.

I'm not sure that starting "contemporary Christian music" was the right thing to do. There's no question that God has used this music to change lives and strengthen His church, and for this reason, maybe it hasn't been so bad. But the negative side of it is that we Christians have "ghettoized" ourselves, almost making ourselves irrelevant to the music mainstream, with the exception of a few "break-out" mainstream hits now and then. We've had far too little impact on the culture at large.

We are called to reach the world, not just those who willingly sit in church pews. That means we are called to preach. If it's necessary, we can use words, but the best sermons are often quietly lived out.

CHAPTER 8

FREAKIN' OUT

SINCE MY FAMILY lives out in the country, we've had an ongoing ant problem in our house. At various times of the year, our home is literally invaded by these creatures. They find their way into everything. One time I poured out a bowl of Cheerios, and as soon as I added the milk, I saw about half a dozen ants trying to swim to the edge of the bowl.

My wife is a purist. To her, exterminators wreak more havoc than they solve. She makes sure that our kids eat right, and she certainly doesn't like the thought of "poisoning" the ants with chemical remedies. That's because to poison the ants, you have to poison the air. Consequently, Deb's a fan of natural, environmental-friendly approaches. The only problem is, none of them work.

Finally, one morning I had had enough. "Look, Deb," I said, "I don't care what we have to do. I don't care how much it costs. I'll sell my car. I'll take out a mortgage on the house. I'll get out of the music business. Whatever it takes, *kill the ants!*"

Deb relented, went to Home Depot, and bought the "poison." We had an ant-free home . . . for all of seven days.

A week later, one of my kids found an ant in his soup. He went berserk. "There's an ant in my soup! Unbelievable! Unbelievable! What's going on in this house?! We've got bugs everywhere. Spiders, centipedes, they're taking over this place!"

"Hey," I said, "It's not the end of the world. It's okay to be upset, but just be careful about the way you respond. An ant in your soup shouldn't make you flip out."

I didn't bring it up at the time because my son has heard it enough, but one of the reasons our kids have bugs in their rooms is because they are always bringing food into their bedrooms! If you've got an opened Pepsi can and an unfinished sandwich lying around, unless you live on the moon, you're gonna have bugs. Guaranteed.

While bugs are a nuisance, they're not the end of the world. Cassie's martyrdom calls us back to the things that matter. When kids are getting shot because of their faith, worrying about a few bugs seems so unimportant. One of the realities of the

Columbine tragedy is that we no longer take normalcy for granted. Parents don't just assume that everything will be okay when they drop their kids off at school. Suddenly, moms are holding school-focused prayer groups, and their kids' safety is one of their primary prayers. Teens are suddenly taking a new look at life as well. When you've faced death, the "little" things of life suddenly seem, well, *little*.

THE THINGS THAT MATTER MOST

I've talked to plenty of teens with serious problems—home lives that really are a mess, with abusive or alcoholic parents. But I've also spoken with a number of teens who don't realize how comfortable their world is. To them, the world revolves around fashion, fashion, fashion.

Now, I'm not one of the "unenlightened" who thinks fashion doesn't matter at all. I don't want to look like I'm clueless when I walk out of the house any more than you do. But there's a line that can be crossed, when our pursuit of fashion overtakes our concern with living out our Christian faith. If you're more concerned with getting the right pair of shoes than with seeing a close friend become a Christian, your priorities are whacked.

Fashion has its merits, but don't make it more important than it is. Keep your priorities in line so that you truly care about the things that matter most.

Peter said that a Christian's beauty "should not come from outward adornment, such as braided hair and the wearing of gold jewelry and fine clothes. Instead, it should be that of your inner self, the unfading beauty of a gentle and quiet spirit, which is of great worth in God's sight" (1 Peter 3:3–4, NIV).

Does this mean it's wrong to wear a ring? Of course not, but it does mean we shouldn't put our identity into jewelry. We shouldn't depend on outward appearance to make us feel like we count.

The same principle holds true for other matters, like worrying about money. I'll admit it—I make a pretty good living. But there was a time in my life when things got so bad that my mom just about refused to stay in my apartment.

My parents came to visit me in Nashville when I was still trying to break into the music business. In those days, I had to move about a dozen times over the course of two years just to get by. One of the places I landed had a little problem with mice, so when my parents came out to hear me sing, I asked my dad to set out some traps. I thought it was a little bit excessive when he set up four, but he said, "You never know."

When we got back to my apartment after the concert, every trap was filled with a dead mouse. My dad was surprised and decided to put four new traps out before we went to bed.

The lights were off for less than ten minutes when we heard, "Bam! Bam! Bam! Bam!"

All four traps sprang shut, catching four more mice. My mom refused to get out of bed until we had all the lights on!

I no longer have to worry about paying the rent, of course, but I've also learned that having a lot of things doesn't satisfy the soul. There are a lot of very lonely people behind the doors of very large mansions.

Jesus said it best:

Do not worry about your life, what you will eat or what you will drink; nor about your body, what you will put on. Is not life more than food and the body more than clothing? . . . Your heavenly Father knows that you need all these things. But seek first the kingdom of God and His righteousness, and all these things shall be added to you. (Matt. 6:25, 32–33 NKJV)

Maybe you didn't get the part you were hoping for in the school play. Maybe you lost first chair in the band, or you didn't get asked to the prom, or any number of things. If you're an adult, maybe you lost a job you really loved or wrecked a favorite car. Keep these disappointments in perspective.

I think back to the paralyzed student I saw at the hospital after the Columbine memorial service. Her life has been radically changed. Instead of complaining about ants in her soup, she'd be delighted if she could move her own hands to take the ants out. While I'm sure she would be disappointed about not being asked to the prom, I bet she'd be satisfied if she could even dance by herself—as long as her legs would move.

Before you freak out, ask yourself, *Considering what others have faced, is it really that bad?*

CHAPTER 9

FINDING A PLACE TO LIVE YOUR TIME

IN THE LATE eighties, Phil Jackson was going through somewhat of a vocational crisis. His basketball-playing days were over, and he wanted to coach, but there wasn't an owner in the league who wanted him as their head guy. Phil was sort of an uncomfortable, sixties-style hippie living in the business-booming eighties. Since he was somewhat esoteric (when trying to explain President Ronald Reagan's success with voters, Jackson, a liberal Democrat, suggested that it was "the smell. Whatever it was, Reagan had the smell."), owners had a difficult time imagining him putting together a winning team.

Consequently, Jackson did what many middle-aged men do when facing a career crisis—they go for career counseling, which usually involves taking a test that matches your skills and desires with the most suitable profession. I can just imagine the look on Phil's face when he got the results. The top two vocations suggested by his personality profile were *housekeeper* and *trail guide*.[1]

In spite of Jackson's inauspicious start, one owner decided to give him a chance—Jerry Krause, the general manager of the Chicago Bulls. Within a decade, Jackson had become one of the most successful head coaches in all of NBA history, taking home a remarkable six championship titles in just nine years with the Bulls.

A lot of young people think that very successful people are born that way. They imagine that the road to success is one easy walk, that the person knew from day one where he or she was headed.

Sometimes, that might be the case. But far more often, people struggle to find their place so that they can live out their time. Cassie was in this group. About a year before her death, Cassie wrote to her good friend Cassandra:

> I wonder what God is going to do with my life. Like my purpose. Some people become missionaries and things, but what about me? What does God have in store for me? Where do my talents and gifts lie? For now, I'll just take it day by day.

I'm confident that I'll know someday. Maybe I'll look back at my life and think, 'Oh, so that was it!' Isn't it amazing, this plan we're part of?[2]

If only Cassie had known what God had in store for her!

This is the theme of my song "Place in This World." It's an enduring message, because part of living out your time means finding the right place to do it, and that's not always easy. I believe that everyone is born with a particular gift. Not everyone knows what this gift is, but God has given you something, some way of bringing glory to His name. You may not know what you have to give, but it's even more important for you to know that you *do* have something to give. In time, God will reveal it.

A lot of kids tell me they think God wants them in the music business. My answer has two parts: If God has really called you to do this, go for it, knock down the doors, and don't give up. But the second part is this: Be open to having God change your desires and motives. What if you're not supposed to record, but focus on leading worship at your church? Are you willing to do that?

In my own life, I was confident that the music business was where God wanted me, *but I was always willing to do something different.* I still feel that way. If God said it was time to move out of the record business, I'd be gone tomorrow.

In fact, I live with a number of unfulfilled dreams. I've toyed with the thought of acting, preaching, scoring a film, or launching my own film production company. These can be good ambitions, strategic windows into reaching our culture, but I know that the time isn't right for me to vigorously pursue them, so I live without the desire eating me up inside. I'm content to be where I am, because I know this is exactly where God wants me to be.

There's a major difference between *mission* and *ambition.* Are you pursuing your dream because that's what God wants you to do, or are you pursuing it just because that's what *you* want to do? Both can go together, of course. I certainly wanted to play music, and I believed God wanted me to as well. But I held my dreams with an open hand. I was willing to let God take them back, because I knew that making records wouldn't fulfill me; only obedience to God's will can do that.

I make a great living and I love what I do, but none of that brings me any peace. Making a hit doesn't bring peace; having a big bank account doesn't bring any peace; and peace is what most of us are after. Peace can be found only within, in a relationship with God. In fact, I derive most of the meaning in my life not by things I've accomplished, but through the people I love. I was asked one time how I felt about winning the Artist of the Year Award in 1999. The honest truth was that I had forgotten all about the award! There are many days I never even think about it; if reporters didn't keep asking me about it, my recollections would be few and far between.

But I never forget I'm a dad. I *never* forget I'm a husband. These are the things that I cherish on an hourly basis.

FINDING YOUR PLACE

George Muller, a famous prayer warrior who founded and directed a faith-based orphanage, once said that 90 percent of finding God's will is having no will of our own. Once we throw our lives into God's plan and purposes, what we should do becomes much more clear. But there are other steps we can take.

In his book, *Finding the Will of God,* Bruce Waltke gives a helpful six-part test.[3] He urges us away from doing things like "putting out a fleece." If you remember the biblical story of Gideon, you'll recall that God asked Gideon to go into battle. Wanting to make sure that God was speaking to him, Gideon put out a sheep's fleece overnight and asked God to make the ground dry but the fleece wet with dew. When he woke up, the ground was perfectly dry but Gideon was able to wring a bucket's worth of water out of the fleece.

Still not sure, Gideon decided to hedge his bets and asked God to make the ground wet and the fleece dry. When he woke up the next morning, it was exactly as he had prayed. There could be no doubting God's will now.

Today, many Christians do something similar. They pray, "God, I'll know you're calling me to go on a summer's mission trip if so-and-so calls me this evening." We set up little tests to see if God will lead us in any one particular direction.

The main problem with this is that the Bible presents God as being *patient* with Gideon, but nowhere does it suggest that Gideon's request is a model for how we should make decisions. In fact, the whole scope of the Bible pushes us away from making decisions this way. The book of Proverbs urges us to get "wisdom" and "understanding," two far more valuable tools than setting out a fleece.

Waltke says a more biblical way to make decisions is adopting a long-term, six-step process. First, *we need to read our Bible constantly*. This trains our minds to think biblically. There's no shortcut here. By reading God's Word, we get a better understanding of His principles and His wisdom. You can't get all this in one quick reading, or by furiously looking up a subject in the concordance, hoping that God will somehow mystically speak through the Bible. It takes time to have our character gradually transformed to agree with the truth of Scripture.

Second, *once we have begun training ourselves with Scripture and prayer, we will begin developing a heart that is close to God*. Out of this heart, we can discern God's leading. This makes sense, doesn't it? If God gives us His heart, we are actually following *Him* when we follow that heart's longings. But again, this takes time. In the meantime, we can discern God's will through the third step: *receiving wise counsel.*

One of the reasons people ask me about how to break into the music business is because I've been there and they think I might know something they don't. The same thing is true in all walks of life. We need the sound input of wiser, more experienced people.

The fourth step to determine God's will is *to look for God's providence.* Is God opening the doors for you, or are all the doors slamming shut? Sometimes you have to open a lot of slammed doors, but if God is leading you, eventually the right door will open.

Fifth, we can *apply sound judgment.* We do this by simply asking ourselves, "Does this decision make sense?" Ask yourself: Does your decision square with scriptural teaching? Are you gifted in the area you want to pursue? Will your circumstances allow you to pursue this track? Does it make sense in light of your overall life strategy and calling?

Finally, the sixth step is *willingly accepting divine intervention.* Most often, God will guide us through the first five steps, giving us a lot of freedom to choose within that realm. If you want to play music for a living, if your heart keeps leading you in that direction, and if you're gifted enough to put together music that people like to listen to, then you're probably free to pursue that career. But are you willing to have God step in and block the way, redirecting you in some other direction?

Misty and Brad Bernall had a tough decision to make when they considered whether to take Cassie out of private school and let her attend Columbine. Eventually, that decision put Cassie in a place where her life was taken away. But that decision also led to a tremendous witness to the entire world.

All of us probably wonder, at least from time to time, what God really wants us to do. Sometimes we ask this question just because we're tired or bored with what we're already doing. Other times it's because we don't yet have the life-experience we need to discover just what it is God is calling us to do.

Be patient with yourself. Hold your unfulfilled dreams with an open hand. I've found it most helpful to take George Muller's advice and work to get rid of my own will, so that God's will can be done.

Ultimately, it's not what we *do* that brings peace and fulfillment. It's who we *are* and who we *love*. Build up those areas of your life, and you'll certainly find your place in this world.

CHAPTER 10

COACH

"NICE JOB. THAT was a good pass."

"Get your feet set."

"Look out for the blitz! Look out for the blitz!"

Jim Zorn was the Seattle Seahawks' all-time leading passer. Now in his late forties, he is too old to still play football, but you can see him on the Detroit Lions' sideline, giving instant advice to the team's quarterback via radio. He's what they call a quarterback coach, and his only job is to help one player get just a little bit better.

Even the most experienced quarterbacks have coaches. You may never have heard of Mike McCarthy, but you've probably heard of his pro-tégée: Green Bay quarterback Brett Favre.

Imagine what your life would be like with a personal coach, someone whose only job is to make you perform to the best of your ability; someone who could whisper advice to you in tight situations; someone who has been there and can warn you about the perils you might face.

If NFL quarterbacks, most of whom get paid millions of dollars based on their ability to perform, still need a coach to help them do their best, how much more so do you and I?

This is your time—but that doesn't mean you have to go it alone. You'll go much further and make fewer mistakes if you find a personal coach. Ideally, you have such a coach in your parents. They've been there. They know you like nobody else does—even though sometimes it may not feel like it.

My parents are definitely role models in my life. The main reason I was able to stand against the partying crowd was because I received the acceptance I needed at home. "Fitting in" still mattered, but I didn't crave it like some others did. I knew my parents loved me, and I respected the way they lived their lives. They stuck with me through the hard times and demonstrated a consistent, unconditional love so that I never strayed so far that I lost my way.

But some of you don't have a real relationship with either parent. Maybe you can find a pastor, or youth leader, or just a trusted older friend who is willing to spend some time to help you become your best.

Another spiritual mentor of mine is Don Finto, my pastor for eighteen years. Don has seen some rough times, but he has changed my life, spiritually. Is there a pastor you know who will spend time with you?

Billy Graham is a role model for me, too. I don't know why Billy and his wife, Ruth, have been so gracious to Deb and me, but I'm thankful that they have been. Billy has sort of taken me under his wing and talked to me about things he wishes he had done differently in his life.

He also shared with me how he has maintained a life of integrity. When you're in the public eye, there are often temptations that others may not realize. Billy's integrity didn't happen by accident. He learned to let men from his team search his hotel room before he checked in. They looked under the beds and in closets, making sure there weren't any problems or potential problems. When Billy told me this, I realized just how much he hungers and thirsts after righteousness.

Just being around Billy and Ruth is inspiring. In 1996, Ruth had some surgery. I was performing near where they live, so we stopped by to see how she was doing. Much to our surprise, Ruth insisted that everybody come into her room. She looked amazing, especially considering what she had just gone through. There wasn't a hair out of place on her head, and she was in very good spirits.

"Michael, will you play for me?" she asked.

How could I say no? I sat down at the piano and started banging out a few songs. My parents were with us, and I noticed tears welling up in my mother's eyes.

"Mom, what's up?" I asked her later.

"I still remember listening to you playing hymns when you were five years old," she said. "You used one finger back then. Never in my wildest dreams did I imagine listening to you play in Billy and Ruth Graham's home."

Billy's ministry has had a major impact on my life. He has asked me to play at many of his crusades, which I'm always eager to do. My assistant knows that I'll go wherever Billy wants me to go, no questions asked.

One time, I played for Billy at a Charlotte, North Carolina, crusade. The stadium was packed, even though the weather was atrocious. A malicious rain pelted the crowd, almost like it had an attitude and wanted to cut people up.

DC Talk played first, and the rain continued throughout their entire show. I played next, and the rain showed no sign of letting up. Then Billy Graham was introduced, and as if on cue, the rain stopped—for about thirty minutes. The second Billy was done preaching, the rain started up again.

Let me tell you, it was hard not to be in awe at that moment.

HOW CAN I SERVE YOU?

Another of my mentors was Bob Briner, author of one of my all-time favorite books, *Roaring Lambs*. I don't think there's a single word in that book I disagree with. Bob makes a strong case for Christians to break out of their subculture and get involved in strategic careers such as journalism, screenwriting, and moviemaking. When I read the book for the first time, I freaked out—it was almost uncanny how much Bob and I see eye to eye. I could tell he was a kindred spirit, even though I hadn't met him.

I finally got to meet him when he came through

Nashville. We immediately hit it off and began a close friendship. I wrote a foreword for one of his books, and we did radio programs together. He E-mailed me all the time and sent numerous faxes, and the communications always contained the attitude, if not the words, "Michael, how can I serve you?"

In 1998, Bob started feeling pretty sick. He went to the doctor, who eventually discovered that he had a grapefruit-sized tumor. Immediate surgery was recommended, and the doctors were able to remove most—but not all—of the cancer. Bob then endured a grueling round of chemotherapy, but ultimately, it was a fight he would lose.

I saw him just two weeks before he died. Chemotherapy is a vicious cure; it exacts a tremendous toll on the body and is about as severe a treatment as you can endure. My friend looked half his normal size as he lay in his hospital bed. He rallied when I walked in, but after just fifteen minutes of praying and talking, I could practically see the color draining out of his face. Bob was exhausted and he needed his rest, so I said I should be leaving.

As I turned to go, I heard Bob say in a weak voice, "Hey, Michael W."

I turned back, and Bob asked, "How can I serve you?"

I was overcome by this man's servant heart. He had just days left to live, but right until the very end he was determined to use them to serve others. Bob taught me a lot about what it means to be a Christian.

WHO'S YOUR COACH?

Who's *your* coach? Who is going to help you find your way and prepare you to live your life when it's your time?

It may be that you can't think of any one individual. Cassie Bernall read a lot of books. She let authors "tutor" her in her final years, underlining their words, taking them to heart, learning what she could.

Whatever works for you, go for it. Find your influence. This may be your time, but you'll go much further if you choose to learn from others as you live it.

CHAPTER 11

WHO ARE YOU LIVING FOR?

CRAIG CABANISS, SENIOR pastor of Grace Church in San Diego, California, tells a true story about his toddler son, whom he caught joyfully singing the word *Alleluia* as he ascended the stairs of their home. As the young boy climbed, his volume increased and the chorus he sang gained momentum. Craig was impressed with his son's ability to vary his note selection. Immediately his mind began to fill with the potential of this newly demonstrated skill. Perhaps his boy would lead worship for assembled thousands; maybe he'd write praise songs that would one day be considered classics; who knows, the boy might even land a recording contract.

Craig was suddenly cast back to reality when his son reached the top stair and built up a *crescendo* for his grand finale. His tiny lungs filled with air and then his voice belted out, *"Alleluia . . . tooooo . . . meeeee!"*

In Craig's words: "His career was over. Another

sad casualty of indwelling sin and poor doctrine."[1]

When your moment comes, you'll have to ask yourself, *Who am I living for?*

One of the most famous names in American business during the eighties and nineties is undoubtedly Donald Trump. "The Donald" has made his mark by always naming his businesses and buildings after himself: Trump Tower, Trump Parc, the Trump Shuttle, Trump's Castle, and the Trump Taj Mahal casino, among others. It seems clear who he is living for.

Cassie Bernall didn't die with her own name on her lips. She died affirming the name of Jesus. She didn't live so that she would be remembered. She lived so that others might remember Jesus' name.

When your friends look at what you say and do, whose kingdom would they think you're building? Your own, or someone else's?

When you wake up in the morning, what drives you more than anything else? Is it a dream that you'll score the winning touchdown? Get your name in the paper? Graduate at the top of your class? Become famous?

None of that will last. Fifty years from now, I

won't care if people remember who Michael W. Smith was, but I'll care very much whether I hear those words from my Savior, "Well done, thou good and faithful servant . . ."

KEEPING IT PERSONAL

When I got the call telling me that "This Is Your Time" had set a record in album sales, I immediately told Deb.

"Okay, but don't get the big head," she said. She was kidding but also kind of serious. She didn't want me to lose touch with reality, and I appreciate that. Of course I was excited and grateful—who wouldn't be? But I went to sleep and forgot all about it. A year from now, or maybe even sooner, I'm sure someone will come along and set a new record.

It's admirable to pursue excellence, though sometimes you're going to face some temptations along the way. I'm in a business that tends to promote the person as much as the work. When you buy a faucet, you don't have any idea who made it, but when you buy a record, you know who the singer is. That's just the nature of what I do.

It's the same for many others. Baseball player Ken Griffey Jr. used to have a banner with his picture on it that covered half of the Seattle Kingdome. You could tell who was on that banner from I-5, one of the busiest highways in the nation. Many professions require some type of self-promotion; otherwise, they wouldn't get any business.

Yet Jesus provided penetrating insight when he watched a group of men "jockey for position" as they sought to sit near Him during a dinner:

> When someone invites you to a wedding feast, do not take the place of honor, for a person more distinguished than you may have been invited. If so, the host who invited both of you will come and say to you, 'Give this man your seat.' Then, humiliated, you will have to take the least important place. But when you are invited, take the lowest place, so that when your host comes, he will say to you, 'Friend, move up to a better place.' Then you will be honored in the presence of all your fellow guests. For everyone who exalts himself will be humbled, and he who humbles himself will be exalted. (Luke 14:8-11 NIV)

What Jesus was saying here is that we shouldn't scratch and claw to fight our way to the top. We shouldn't join in the contest to exalt ourselves over everyone else. Besides, Jesus said, exalting ourselves is a losing game anyway, usually resulting in humiliation and shame more than in honor.

Instead of trying to build up our own name, we should act like servants who focus on meeting the needs of others. We should willingly put ourselves last. The net result will be that God will lift us up.

When I do a concert, I don't want my focus to be on convincing people that I'm maybe the best singer or musician out there. We end many of our concerts with worship because I want people to leave the place with a heart check: Where am I with God?

I play in some places where just doing worship songs wouldn't be appropriate, but even here, we're serving the needs of the people who are sponsoring us to be there. I want to be a servant. I want to serve God with the music I create, and I want to serve those who come to my concerts by giving them something positive and entertaining to listen to and encourage them in their life.

Jesus said that when we act this way, something strange happens. The servant ends up getting the best seat. Notice that Jesus didn't tell us to *refuse* the place of honor. He just says we shouldn't crave it or assume it on our own. If God brings us up to the best seat, the proper response is "Thank you." We recognize that it was God who brought this favor and blessing our way. God has certainly blessed me with various positions in the charts, but getting to the top of those charts has never been my motivation.

In our day-to-day lives, how can we learn to act more like servants? We can do three things: (1) learn to keep a proper perspective; (2) focus our security on the right place; and (3) embrace humility.

KEEP YOUR PERSPECTIVE

By God's grace, I've had number-one hits, albums that went gold and platinum, annual awards, the whole works. If you had told me when I was nineteen that one day I'd have the career I'm having now, I'm sure I would have been ecstatic—and probably too young to handle it well.

But now I know that at the end of the day, none

of that brings peace. Don't get me wrong. I'm a "go-getter." I'm competitive, and I love to win, but I also know that if I lose my perspective and focus on the wrong things, my life will get off track.

When the day is over, what matters is whether I've been faithful to my God first and my family second. Anything else—including building up a name for myself—is wasted effort. It won't last.

FOCUS YOUR SECURITY

There's a big difference between being grateful for success and being obsessed with success. Some people base their self-worth on how well they do something. Their security is in what they accomplish. That's a very slippery road to drive on.

The Bible teaches us that our security isn't based on what we do, but on what Christ has done. Because of Jesus' death on the cross, we've become God's children! I would rather be a peasant and be a child of God than the wealthiest businessman who doesn't know God. I would rather be a paralyzed child of God than the best athlete in Olympic history who doesn't know God.

My destiny isn't defined by what I do but by *who*

I am. The fact that I make records for a living isn't important; what Jesus has done on my behalf is.

Your future doesn't depend on getting the right job, finding the right mate, or earning the right paycheck. The most important part of your future depends on your relationship to Jesus Christ. That's what will define you for all eternity. Ten thousand years from now, none of us will care how much money we made or how famous we were; we'll all be on our knees, in awe of *God's* glory and rejoicing in the name of Jesus.

EMBRACE HUMILITY

One of my managers, Mike Blanton, told me about an executive retreat he attended for the Gaylord corporation, a billion-dollar business. It seems like the Gaylords own half of Nashville. Nobody could dispute whether they've "made" it; they are one of the most successful business enterprises in history.

Yet Mike heard E. K. Gaylord, the chief executive, say to his subordinates, "You know what? Ultimately, you guys don't work for me. Yeah, I sign your paychecks, but you really work for the guy upstairs." I was amazed that a top-level executive would tell his managers that their first allegiance is to God. Gaylord went on: "Let's make millions of dollars *so we can give it away and impact people's lives in a positive way.*"

This is humility: using the strengths and resources God has given us to serve others. It models exactly the spirit of Christ. In John 13, the story of the Last Supper, we read how Jesus knew "the Father had given all things into His hands." There was no identity crisis here; Jesus knew exactly who He was and how powerful He was. He didn't put on a fake front by saying "I'm not really important. I'm not really powerful." Instead, He used His power and position to reach out to others, washing the feet of His disciples.

A lot of Christians have the wrong idea about humility. As Peter Kreeft once said, humility isn't thinking less *of* yourself, it's thinking less *about* yourself. It's not pretending you don't have gifts or strengths; it's using those gifts and strengths to further God's kingdom.

Because of the work I'm in, I'm surrounded by a lot of wealthy and incredibly talented individuals.

What inspires me most, however, is not how much money they make, but what they do with the money they make. It's not how well they can perform, but whom they perform *for*. I hope you surround yourself with friends who put God first.

HEART CHECK

How's your perspective? Is your security based on the right thing? Do you clothe yourself with humility? To find out, ask yourself a few questions:

- What do I daydream about? When I'm lying in my bed or letting my mind wander during the day, do I dream about being famous and wealthy, or am I praying about how I can serve God and love others?

- When I enter a room, am I focused on whether others are noticing me, or whether there's a hurting soul that I need to notice and minister to?

- Is my energy focused on earning earthly or heavenly rewards?

- Is my sense of self-worth dependent on what Jesus has done, or what I've done?

- Am I thankful for what God is doing in my life or bitter about what He's not doing?

By prayerfully asking yourself these questions, you can come pretty close to determining whom you're living for. If it's anything or anyone other than God, please, do yourself a favor and get off that road. It's a dead end. It'll never satisfy. We were created to give God glory and to sing His praises. When we put our best energy and our best efforts into that calling, we won't have time to worry about our own reputation.

CHAPTER 12

FIND A WAY

PEOPLE WHO WANT to do something for God sometimes need to find a way to make the impossible possible.

In October 1999, I was invited to sing a short set before a hockey game that pitted the Nashville Predators against the Atlanta Thrashers. What I didn't know at that time was the story behind the Thrashers' general manager, Don Waddell.

I've never met Don personally, but we're about the same age, and he has a "can-do" spirit that I admire. When he was just sixteen years old, growing up in Detroit, his mom called him from work. Don could immediately tell from his mom's voice that she was pretty upset. Her car had broken down, and since she couldn't afford *not* to go into work, she had just left the vehicle by the side of the road and caught a ride into town.

Imagine Mrs. Waddell's surprise when, a few hours later, Don showed up at her office—by himself—with *both* cars.

How had he done it? Think about it for a moment, and we'll come back to this story later.

The Bible is one long story about how God asked normal, everyday individuals to tackle the impossible. Noah built an ark in a land where there was no body of water big enough to float it. Abraham, married to a barren wife, became the father of a great nation, too numerous to count. Moses took a nation of slaves and freed them from the most powerful ruler on earth. Deborah, a woman, gained renown by leading Israel to victory over the mighty Canaanites. Gideon was told to attack a larger foe, but to do so after leaving most of his army behind.

My own life has a little bit of the impossible. While I picked up music by ear pretty early on in life, there were plenty of doubters. When I was a senior in high school, a well-known piano teacher said I would "never amount to a dime" musically. Early on, when I told my dad I wanted to make an album, he tried to bring me back to reality by asking, "That's just fine, son, but who's going to buy it? You've only got so many friends."

My journey to Nashville took me through a

number of odd jobs as I tried to make a living while breaking into the music industry: in landscaping, with an antiques dealer, at Coca-Cola, in a clothing store—and that was just in one year! I think my parents always knew I'd have something to do with music, but few expected that I'd become a singer. I had my own doubts early on.

But it's happened. I didn't let the "impossible" box me out. That's why I continue to look past obstacles today, including starting a ministry we call Rocketown.

ROCKETOWN

"It'll never work, Michael."

That's all I needed to hear. I love a challenge.

A number of years ago, I went to downtown Franklin, just to "hang" and pray and see what was going on. It wasn't a pleasant sight. Many of the young kids were living for the moment, living for pleasure, living for the next high, living for everything except God's kingdom. Many of them looked hardened beyond their years, as if their souls had been permanently shut off.

God put a strong burden in my heart. "It would be great to get these kids off the street, Lord," I prayed. "What should I do?"

Gradually, the idea for Rocketown, a music club/outreach to kids, started to form in my mind. All the studies said Rocketown was a bad idea. Financially, it looked impossible. Some people thought that purposely drawing in such hardened youth was crazy, like I was intentionally inviting trouble. Other Christian leaders told me, "Look, we've already got Young Life and Teen Challenge; what can Rocketown do that they're not doing? We're already reaching those teens."

"But we're not," I said. I love Young Life. I have great respect for Teen Challenge. But many of the kids who are hanging in downtown Franklin on the weekend wouldn't be caught dead in a Young Life meeting. That's nothing against Young Life; it's just that you can't expect one approach to reach all kinds of kids, and I wanted to reach the hardest, most closed-off teens.

It took three years from the night I spent praying in downtown Franklin to the night when Rocketown opened its doors. Rocketown is one of the most frustrating, challenging, and yet reward-ing ministries I've ever been a part of. The frustrat-ing part came when financial reality set in, and we realized it really would be tough to fund this thing. People like to give money to building campaigns; supporting an outreach to "weird-looking" kids ended up being a much harder sell.

But the rewards came when I'd see God use counselors like Sean Hedegard to break through the hardest heart. It took time; nothing happened fast, but God has blessed the effort. Conventional formulas wouldn't work with these kids. Sean had to get down on his knees and pray, "God show me the way—give me the creativity to find a window into this person's closed heart."

Rocketown was open for three years. Then we had to close the club part for awhile, though we have kept meeting with kids on an individual basis. We needed to find a new place to meet, which wasn't easy. Finally, after three years, Rocketown will reopen in 2000. We have the perfect building in downtown Nashville, and everything is in place to bring it back bigger and better than ever.

I can't lie to you; Rocketown has been a tough

ministry to manage. It has never been "easy," but it's challenges like this that make life worth living. I feel sorry for people who always take the easy route, who give up at the first sign of opposition or trouble.

BUILDING A LIFE

Back to Don Waddell, who managed to deliver two cars to his mom's office. After jump-starting his mom's car, Don drove six blocks and parked it. He then ran back to his car, passed his mom's, and drove for another six blocks, where he parked his car. He got out of his car and ran back to his mom's, repeating the process for the three miles it took to reach his mom's office.

That's determination! And hockey fans knew that a new franchise like the Thrashers would need somebody with that character. "It's an unbelievable task to start a team with a blank sheet of paper," Waddell told *Sports Illustrated*. "I've laid awake many nights wondering, Have I forgotten anything? Heck, three days before training camp we still didn't have any pucks."[1]

What inspires me about Waddell's story is that his character was built early on. He was only sixteen when he found a way to drive two cars to his mom's office. I wonder how many teens would say, "It can't be done." Or perhaps, "Well, I could do what Waddell did, but that would be too much work."

The choices you make today—your creativity, your determination, your drive, your motivation—will shape the person that you become. Use today's challenges to build a character and perseverance that will help you succeed long after the challenge is past.

CHAPTER 13

ORDINARY PEOPLE, EXTRAORDINARY LIVES

HE WAS WHAT sports announcers call, with just a hint of condescension in their voices, a "journeyman." Playing on a team with Mickey Mantle and Yogi Berra, you had to be a superstar to distinguish yourself, and Don Larson, pitcher for the New York Yankees, was anything but that. In fact, as a pitcher he lost more games than he won. During Game Two of the 1956 World Series, Larson pitched so poorly that Yankees manager Casey Stengel took him out in the second inning. (While few starting pitchers last for nine innings, most hope to make it into at least the seventh inning.)

To make matters worse, Larson had to face what may have been one of the best-hitting lineups in baseball history. Included on the Dodgers roster were future Hall of Famers Jackie Robinson, Roy Campanella, Duke Snider, and Pee Wee Reese.

Larson knew he was slated to pitch again in

Game Five. His earlier poor showing had caused a crisis in his confidence, so he did something drastic: he completely discarded his windup and went with a much more direct approach. For a pitcher to so completely change his style in the middle of the World Series is astonishing, but at least early on, it looked like it was working. Larson kept retiring the Dodgers, and then the Yankees finally scored in the fourth inning off a Mickey Mantle solo home run.

As it turned out, that was the only run Don Larson ever needed.

Inning followed inning, and by the sixth, the crowd was unusually excited. Don Larson was pitching a perfect game—no walks, no hits, no base runners of any kind. As the game stretched into the seventh and eighth innings, the contest took on a fevered pitch. Larson had faced and retired twenty-four batters in a row. There was just one inning left.

The first two Dodgers went down, leaving just one player, pinch hitter Dale Mitchell, standing between Don Larson and something that had never been done before: pitching a perfect game in the World Series.

The first pitch was a ball, but the next three pitches brought three straight strikes. Yankees catcher Yogi Berra charged the mound, wrapped his legs around the journeyman, and planted kisses on both his cheeks. A thoroughly "average" player had just given an extraordinary performance. Larson might have lost more games than he won over the course of his career, but on the day it mattered most, he was literally perfect.

Some athletes, on the other hand, seem born to achieve extraordinary results. During a 1999 interview on Dallas's KTCK radio, Ken Griffey Jr. talked about his friendship with Tiger Woods. Like many others, I became fascinated with Tiger during his rookie pro season in 1997, when he won the Masters tournament by a phenomenal twelve strokes. I love playing golf, and like many golf fans, I've been in awe of Tiger's success.

Griffey—himself a world-renowned athlete— was equally in awe. He recounted how Tiger decided to play a par 5 hole (for those of you who don't golf, par 5 means it's a *long* way from the tee to the cup) *on his knees.* Tiger hit every shot kneeling down—*and still parred the hole!*[1]

Most of us will never experience the level of mastery that Tiger has demonstrated with a golf club. We live far more ordinary lives and are forced to make our way much more slowly. That's why Don Larson's story inspires me so much; his is the pattern of life that Cassie Bernall fit into: an "ordinary" person achieving something special.

Though Cassie Bernall's life is now extraordinary, she wasn't a young woman who stood out from the crowd even a year before her death. Cassie's youth group leader, Dave, told Misty, "Some of the kids in the youth group are A-plus personalities: they can talk, they can dance, they're the life of every party. Cassie was not. But she still hung in there. And that's why she was a hero to me—because I see Cassies every day, year after year, and so many of them just give up."[2]

Only days before the Columbine shootings, Cassie was just an "average" teen, living out her faith during the tumultuous teen years. And yet, just as it seems that Tiger was born to play golf, so Cassie's mother, Misty, believes Cassie was born to witness about Jesus Christ during this nation's worst school-related tragedy.

I talk to a lot of young people who feel trapped by being average. They want to stand out, but they just barely make the team, have an okay voice, get a B average, and never really excel at any one particular thing.

You know what? Few people remember Don Larson's overall record, but every serious baseball buff could tell you who he was and what he did. His memory isn't defined by his average years, but by that one extraordinary accomplishment. You never know what God has in store for you!

ETERNAL REWARDS

I'm not suggesting that every faithful Christian will be world-famous for fifteen minutes. Actually, I'm saying something much more awesome. Every faithful Christian will be honored by God for eternity.

Jesus talked a lot about receiving heavenly rewards. In Matthew 5:12, He said of those of us who face persecution on His behalf (certainly Cassie fits this description), "great is your reward in heaven." In Matthew 6:1–4, He promised us that God sees our "average" secret deeds, and that He will reward us accordingly, urging us to "lay up for yourselves treasures in heaven" (Matt. 6:20). It's a dead-end street to pursue fame on this earth, but it's a solid investment to seek after heavenly rewards. Even Tiger Woods's trophies will eventually rust and decay. The money he's earned will eventually be spent, and sometime in the future, another exciting young player will take Tiger's place as the biggest thing on the PGA Tour.

The treasures we lay up for ourselves in heaven—the kind that Cassie stashed away just before she left this earth—will always be with us. And most of the rewards that Jesus talked about don't come from extraordinary achievements. He mentioned the quiet things: giving our money to God's work, feeding the hungry, visiting those in prison, being faithful on a daily basis.

When you get to heaven, I guarantee you that God won't ask you about your batting average or your golf handicap. But He may bring up the Compassion International child you sponsored.[3] He probably will mention the non-Christians you took the time to witness to. And in that moment, your "average" life will suddenly become extraordinary, because there's no such thing as "average" when faith in Jesus Christ is added to the equation.

CHAPTER 14

SUDDEN STORMS

ONE HUNDRED YEARS ago Galveston, Texas, had more millionaires per square mile than the far more fashionable and trendy city of Newport, Rhode Island. It was the beginning of the century, a time of optimism when humankind was gradually overcoming more and more barriers. George Eastman's camera had brought the realm of photography from the experts to the amateurs. Thomas Edison had captured the first reproduced sound, making a "record" out of tin foil. Transportation was on the verge of a major revolution: by 1903, the Wright brothers would fly. By 1908, Henry Ford produced the prototype Model T.

Other sciences were not quite so advanced, but even so, confidence remained high. For example, weather experts were convinced that storms rising out of the Caribbean would arc north and east up the Atlantic coast, leaving the exposed Galveston coast free of concern. At least, that was the dogged opinion of Isaac M. Cline, chief of the United

States Weather Bureau's Galveston station.

A few people suggested that perhaps a storm could wipe out Galveston's vulnerable shores. Since Galveston is surrounded by water on three sides, making it little more than a sand island, a severe storm could conceivably obliterate it. But, filled with the optimism of advancement in 1900, Cline boldly proclaimed, "The opinion . . . that Galveston will at some time be seriously damaged by some such disturbance, is simply an absurd delusion."[1]

To make matters worse, Cline was so confident of his opinion that he stopped all telegraphed weather communications from Cuba during the height of the 1900 hurricane season. He thought he didn't need the forewarning of "excitable Latins."

One week later, Havana's Belén Observatory warned of a hurricane on track to hit central Texas. Had this warning been acted upon, there would have been plenty of time for Galveston to be evacuated, but Cline paid no attention, certain that the storm would travel north up the Atlantic coast as he had predicted.

Cline couldn't have been more wrong, and the

results were almost apocalyptic. The geography of the Gulf of Mexico and Galveston Bay is such that the hurricane piled up waters and sent a terrifying surge blasting into Galveston's wealthy, confident community on September 8. Because people were so self-assured, they hadn't taken care to prepare. Items that weren't tied down were picked up by the wind and became giant shrapnel, fatally wounding terrified citizens who ventured outside to see what was going on. The unique tidal wave that formed carried a steamship for *two miles* inland before laying the vessel down. By the time the storm had passed, between six and eight thousand people had perished. The storm of 1900 is the United States's worst weather-related loss of life in history.

Today, we are well-warned about such "physical" storms. When Hurricane Floyd threatened to pummel the east coast in the fall of 1999, various state and federal authorities organized the United States's largest peacetime evacuation ever. Residents whose homes and communities were threatened could literally watch the storm's progress over the Internet. Though early reporting varied, by the time the storm came within striking distance, experts had a good idea of where the storm would land, and when. Consequently, the initial loss of life, relatively speaking, was very small, and many of those who died were victims of the flooding that *followed* the storm.

Though modern science can forewarn us about physical storms, none of us can predict "social" storms. When the students at Columbine left their houses on April 20, 1999, they didn't have a clue about what was going to happen. School officials and classmates were caught totally by surprise. There was no way they could know what was about to happen.

Odds are that, eventually, you'll face a "sudden storm" of your own. Deb and I faced a particularly scary one when our son Ryan was just seven.

SICK BOY

"Your son is a very sick boy," the doctor told my family. When Deb's mom relayed the news, my jaw dropped open. *This is not happening!* I wanted to shout.

But it was.

Ryan is our oldest child; those of you who have kids are fully aware of how little first-time parents really know. It's your first time around, after all, so you can be caught by surprise.

At the time of the doctor's diagnosis, Deb and I were in our early thirties; my career was just taking off, and life looked pretty smooth up ahead. Then Ryan started blinking his eyes in bizarre ways. Sometimes, we'd notice tics—he'd jerk his head around and twitch. Occasionally, he'd even fall to the floor and shake.

This behavior seemed so weird that at first Deb and I didn't know what to make of it. Initially, we thought he was just incredibly hyper. Ryan was, after all, a very active boy. But the twitching and shaking got so bad we thought we'd better see a doctor.

That's when we heard the shocking words, "Your son is a very sick boy."

Deb and I were devastated. The doctor said Ryan suffered from Tourette's syndrome, a neurological disorder infamous for its involuntary body movements and, in some cases, spontaneous obscene outbursts (something which Ryan never did). It's more common in boys than in girls, and often appears in childhood. The worst part was the doctor's prognosis. Tourette's syndrome often grows *worse* as a person ages.

Deb and I received the news in shock. Deb started crying, and I held her, thinking, *This is not happening. This cannot be happening.*

After grieving for a few days, we decided to not just accept the doctor's diagnosis. Instead, we invited prayer teams to come to our house and pray for Ryan. We anointed him, we anointed his bedroom, we prayed, we fasted, we did everything we could think of.

Ultimately, however, we knew that the entire situation was in God's hands. There wasn't anything more we could do.

We took Ryan to another doctor, who looked Ryan over and said, "This boy doesn't have Tourette's. He's extremely creative, a little hyper, maybe even brilliant, but he doesn't have Tourette's. It looks to me like he's already a young man living in a boy's body. About 10 percent of boys experience twitching at his age. In almost all the cases, it passes as they get older, and I think that's the case here."

Whether Ryan was healed, or whether the second doctor was correct and Ryan just outgrew it, our son no longer has any of the symptoms that he used to. About three and a half years after he first started twitching, the episodes stopped.

Our sudden storm was over.

SHELTER IN THE STORM

I'm not sure that you can prepare yourself for storms like the one I just described. Certainly, Cassie couldn't prepare herself for facing down a gunman. Sudden storms are part of life that test our ability to trust God. Since we can't fully prepare, we are forced to rest in God's preparation. God knows how to prepare us. He can build us up into the people we'll need to be in order to pass the test.

The life preserver for Deb and me as we faced Ryan's situation was trust. We looked at each other and said, "You know what? God is going to get us through this. No matter what happens, God will provide the strength we need."

The Bible promises me that God won't put me through anything I can't bear:

No temptation has overtaken you except such as is common to man; but God is faithful, who will not allow you to be tempted beyond what you are able, but with the temptation will also make the way of escape, that you may be able to bear it. (1 Cor. 10:13 NKJV)

The word translated "temptation" here is *peirasmos* in the Greek. It doesn't necessarily mean temptation; it can also mean a test or a trial, and most commentators believe that in this passage, both meanings come into play.

Paul gave us two concrete, you-can-bet-your-life-on-it assurances for whenever we face these tests. The first promise is based on the faithfulness of God—what I call "the trust factor." Regardless of the test, Paul said, God is faithful. He won't let us be tried to such an extent that we can't endure it. God is in control. Our heavenly Father regulates everything that happens to us. He knows what we can handle based on the strength He provides, and He won't let anything come our way that exceeds that threshold.

The second assurance is that in every trial, God

gives us a "way of escape that you may be able to bear it." At first this sounds a little weird. Why do we need to bear a trial if God is providing a way of escape? Well, the way of escape might be delayed. Deb and I had to wait *three and a half years* for Ryan's symptoms to clear up. During that time, God gave us the strength to endure.

I recommend that every Christian memorize 1 Corinthians 10:13. In all honesty, life can be heartlessly cruel. Just read one day's paper, and you'll see the terrible things that can happen and that people do to each other. It can be almost unbelievable.

But God is always believable. God's power can help us overcome a cruel world. Cruel things may still happen to us, but if they do, we know first that God will be faithful to us in the midst of that trial, and second, that eventually He'll provide a way of escape.

Val Schnurr's "escape" is having to endure a lengthy period of recovery. Val will bear some scars and discomforts for the rest of her life, but God is aware of each one, and He'll help get her through them.

We don't get to choose our particular route of

escape, and that's where the trust factor comes in again. God knows what is best for you. Learn to rest in His will.

HUMILITY IN THE STORM

The unpredictability of life should humble us— and also call us to be more serious about the state of our souls. When I first heard Cassie's story, my reaction to it was the same as her mother's: Would I have said yes? Most of us will never be tested in the way Cassie was, but all of us can grow spiritu- ally, and in the end, our spiritual maturity will help us weather anything that comes our way.

Cassie prepared herself by studying. She read good books, she talked with her Christian friends about how these books might apply to her life, and she prayed for God's strength to live out the truths she was reading.

She also surrounded herself with other Christians. When you read Misty's book, *She Said Yes,* you realize that fitting in with the Christian crowd wasn't particularly easy for Cassie. Even though she didn't believe she fit in, she refused to let awkwardness keep her from doing what she knew was the right thing to do.

As a result, when the sudden storm hit, Cassie was ready. She didn't expect the storm, but when it crashed into her world, she had the internal strength to face it.

We shouldn't fear sudden storms. We know that God will protect us and watch over us. But we should get ready for them. How do we do that?

First, *we need to make friends with Scripture.* Favorite Bible verses should be our best friends, on our lips ready to be recalled whenever we need them. I've made it a practice to memorize numerous Scriptures throughout my life. Some of my favorites are Psalms 138 and 139; Colossians 1:9-6; Romans 8:1; and Jeremiah 29:11.

We can also train ourselves spiritually by *taking risks.* Be willing to live out on the edge, like Rich Mullins. Find somebody whom you think is least likely to be interested in the gospel and befriend them. Win them over with God's love. Stretch yourself. Refuse to always take the easy way out.

Another way that we can prepare ourselves for sudden storms is by *being obedient in mini-storms.*

Don't compromise on your faith. There's no such thing as a minor sin, because every act of rebellion makes our heart just a little bit colder to God.

Finally, I think all of us need *to begin our day with prayer.* We need God's "heads up," His advance warnings, and to get them we have to give Him time and quiet when He can speak into our heart. He can prepare us ahead of time. We can certainly ask for His guidance throughout the day.

Don't be caught unprepared. Sudden storms are inevitable, but God has given us everything we need to prepare ourselves for the worst, and then to hang on when the clouds descend. With His strength, we can pass through the storms stronger in our faith and more committed to our God.

CHAPTER 15

STANDING UP

LILITH FAIR WAS designed to increase exposure for women's music as well as to raise money for various nonprofit organizations. That's an admirable goal, but apparently, the organizers aren't quite as open to "diversity" as they advertise.

When the music fest came to the Blossom Music Center in Cleveland, Ohio, in the summer of 1999, fans were greeted by an unusual display. There were the usual groups of people laughing and talking, sitting in groups on the grass, an occasional guitar player leading a small group in songs, people eating various foods from the many booths that surrounded the grounds.

But then there was a woman standing in front of the National Organization for Women (NOW) booth. Her eyes were covered with sunglasses, her hair was pulled back under a baseball cap—all normal enough—but what made her stand out was the gag in her mouth and the T-shirt she wore that proclaimed, "Peace begins in the womb, Sarah."

The slogan was a call to Sarah McLachlan, the Grammy-winning recording artist who founded the show. The woman wearing the T-shirt was Marilyn Kopp, who claims she has been "gagged" by Lilith Fair organizers. Kopp is the executive director of the Ohio chapter of Feminists for Life of America (FFL), a pro-woman, pro-life group that wasn't allowed to set up booth space in the Lilith Fair Village, an area where assorted activists and vendors set up tables to publicize their organization's activities and products. FFL wasn't allowed to set up a booth because they oppose abortion.

Since Kopp wasn't allowed into the fair the traditional way (as a vendor), she and two other FFL members bought tickets, put on gags, and stood in front of several booths that are known for their abortion advocacy. Their reasoning was that if Lilith Fair really wanted to achieve its goal of trying to "raise consciousness about issues that affect women's lives," they should permit a feminist group that also believes abortion is wrong.

If nothing else, Kopp's stance for the unborn in such a hostile environment is certainly courageous. The women sitting at the NOW and Planned

Parenthood booths were none too happy to have Kopp and her friends standing there. Occasionally, a woman walked by who shouted out her preference for Planned Parenthood's abortion advocacy, but there were also the occasional supportive hugs from like-minded fans who appreciated Kopp's bravery and creativity.

Marilyn Kopp told a Cleveland newspaper that she believed abortion goes against the basic principles of feminists—justice, nonviolence, and nondiscrimination. Abortion, she said, is the product of the oppression society has placed on women; it is the very definition of exploitation. Women should not have to conform to rules in a male society to be successful and accepted. Kopp believes herself to be not only pro-life but also pro-human.

The newspaper took a surprisingly tough stand against Kopp's exclusion. The writer of the article was surprised that a feminist leader like McLachlan would censor other feminists. A group that strongly favors the pro-choice movement should surely include all of the options and opinions and allow women the freedom to decide for themselves.

The newspaper article went on to mention that

there have been surprising results to several recent studies. One study by Faye Wattleton's Center for Gender Equity found the support for the abortion rights movement is decreasing among women.

What I admire about Kopp's approach is her creativity, persistence, and her willingness to preach to a crowd that doesn't normally attend church. She's out there on the front lines, standing up for what she believes in. She's not hollering in a Christian ghetto, buying time for ads on stations where 90 percent of the listeners already agree with her. Far from it. She's standing up where she knows she'll take some hits.

I have to admit, Kopp's style is not my own. I've never been an "in your face" kind of guy. But there's a place to take a courageous and visible stand. We all have our own temperaments and talents and missions before God. There's no "one way" to stand up for God.

Kopp's story also challenges me that sometimes, I don't have to "wait" for an opportunity like Cassie's to make my faith known. Sometimes, we can *create* those opportunities. We can step out with a radical witness and stand up for what we believe in.

THE TIRELESS BELIEVER

It's stunning to realize that when Christ died, the number of Christians could be counted in dozens. Most of Jesus' followers fell away when He was arrested and then crucified. A handful remained publicly visible; a few more kept praying, but they were fearful, locked behind their doors, not sure of what would happen. The fate of Christianity looked very uncertain; it was hanging by an extremely slender thread.

On the day of Pentecost, their numbers swelled by about three thousand. Finally, there were enough believers to constitute an actual religion, but most of the apostles kept the focus of their evangelism on the Jews. They never thought to extend their faith to the rest of the world and certainly not to the Gentiles, at least not until a fiery young man named Paul was struck blind and converted to the faith.

Pentecost was the fire that got Christianity going, but Paul was the flamethrower who spread the fire across the world. His missionary journeys are astonishing, considering how much ground he covered and how many churches he planted. In just ten years—between A.D. 47 and A.D. 57—Paul planted the Christian faith in four provinces of the Roman empire: Galatia, Macedonia, Achaia, and Asia. Before Paul entered these territories, there wasn't a single believer to be found. By the time he left, a viable, growing church was reaching out to the lost.

In spite of imprisonment, beatings, shipwrecks, extreme hunger, and violent opposition, Paul never slowed down. He was zealous for God's work, and he spent the best part of his energies and life promoting God's work in what were then considered foreign lands.

Paul certainly didn't sit back and "hope" that the Gentiles would eventually embrace Jesus Christ. He spent his life creatively reaching out, finding ways to introduce the gospel to each city.

I believe that all of us are called to be as proactive as Paul. Too many people think Christianity is about what you *don't* do, but the faith that Paul lived out is marked by what you *do* do.

It helps to have a larger vision. The best way to become proactive is to catch a vision and then go after it. The people I admire most are the people who live with this sense of destiny.

One such man was Abraham Lincoln. During the Civil War, Lincoln became almost obsessed with one goal: preserving the Union. While some advisers warned him to stop the Civil War and sue for peace with the South, Lincoln refused and fought on. As the death toll mounted, Lincoln's political stock plummeted. In fact, when he went to eulogize the slain soldiers at Gettysburg, one politician snidely remarked, "Let the dead bury the dead."

In 1864, when it looked certain that Lincoln wouldn't be reelected, some of Lincoln's advisers recommended that he declare a national emergency and refuse to hold the election. A power-hungry politician would have delighted to follow such advice, but Lincoln kept a bigger picture in mind.

"We cannot have free government without elections," he said, "and if the rebellion could force us to forgo, or postpone a national election, it might fairly claim to have already conquered and ruined us."[1]

Notice that by going ahead with the election

(which most people thought he would lose), Lincoln put his personal fortunes at risk for the sake of something much more important than his own fame or his own place in history: the greater good of the nation he had pledged to serve.

In August 1864, since it appeared certain that Lincoln would lose the election to General McClellan (who had promised to end the war and recognize the South's claims to independence), Lincoln wrote a memorandum that revealed his iron-clad determination:

> This morning, as for some days past, it seems exceedingly probable that this administration will not be re-elected. Then it will be my duty to so cooperate with the president elect, as to save the Union between the election and the inauguration; as he will have secured his election on such ground that he cannot possibly save it afterwards.[2]

Lincoln was saying that if he lost the election, he would work night and day to win the war before the newly-elected president was inaugurated, since he knew that McClellan would end the war as soon as he took office. All that mattered to Lincoln was keeping this country together, and he was determined to use every last second of his term to do just that. He didn't run for reelection because he couldn't take the thought of not being president. He ran for reelection because he knew another president might give up.

That's vision. That's focus.

I also feel I have a destiny to fulfill. They may not write about me in the history books, but like you, I have something that God wants me to accomplish. At forty-two years old, some might say I'm getting up there for a guy who plays pop music, but my destiny goes beyond making records. In fact, my work has just begun. I don't think I'll ever retire. I may not do seventy-five shows a year, but from a ministry standpoint, I'll always be thinking of ways to spread the gospel.

That's because the more I accomplish, the more I see that needs to be done. After a year in which I grieved with the parents at Columbine, mourned with much of the world at the passing of Payne Stewart, and faced the heartache of losing my mentor and friend, Bob Briner, I'm more convinced than ever that we need to be working day and night to accomplish God's will for our lives—because none of us knows how much longer we have left. I'd better be doing what I'm supposed to be doing, because God might be coming back for me a lot sooner than I realize.

What are you doing to fulfill God's destiny? What vision is driving your life?

CHAPTER 16

RUNNING THE RACE

CASSIE'S RACE IS over. She ran to win, and God gave her the victory. You and I still probably have a few miles to go.

A verse that has really inspired me comes from the book of Hebrews:

> Therefore we also, since we are surrounded by so great a cloud of witnesses, let us lay aside every weight, and the sin which so easily ensnares us, and let us run with endurance the race that is set before us. (Hebrews 12:1 NKJV)

UNDER THE CLOUD

"Okay, here we go. It's going to be a nice ride tonight."

I love it when this feeling comes over me during a concert, but for you to understand what I'm talking about, I'll have to explain it with a bit of Scripture.

In Hebrews 11, leading up to chapter 12, verse 1,

the writer listed the great heroes of our faith, beginning with Abel, going through Noah, Abraham and Sarah, Moses, Joshua and Rahab, and many others. When he said "we are surrounded by so great a cloud of witnesses," I don't know if he meant that these saints are literally watching us, but I do know that sometimes it almost seems like they are.

I experience this sometimes when I'm playing in summer festivals. It's not very easy to play these gigs. Seventy thousand people are running around in a big, outdoor place, and the grounds aren't constructed specifically for bands, so it can be hard to keep everybody together. It's so much easier in a theater, with maybe 3,000 or so fans focused specifically on a stage.

But something almost mystical seems to happen near the end of our set when we launch into praise and worship songs such as "Awesome God" or "Sanctuary." Without fail, something lifts when we start singing these songs. You can feel it. Some nights, you almost think you can see it. It's like the saints of old are behind you, rooting you on, worshiping the Lord with you.

I love it when this happens. I'll usually close my

eyes and think, *Okay, here we go. It's going to be a nice ride tonight.* I'm still playing, but the real work is taking place around me, behind me, and through me, *but not because of me*. I'm just a conduit for something much bigger than me. I know things are happening out there that have nothing to do with my own abilities, but the grace of God's Spirit. People's hearts are being changed; people start weeping; others recommit their hearts to the Lord. We may not hear about these until months later, when someone decides to send us a letter. Some we'll probably never hear about, but it's obvious that God is moving in people's hearts.

The God we serve has been calling men and women to stand up for him for thousands of years. You're not the first one God has called to show courage and faith in a difficult situation, and you won't be the last. Take comfort from the fact that great heroes of the faith are rooting you on, standing there as a witness for your encouragement.

The great Bible commentator F. F. Bruce said that he doubts the word *witness* should be read literally, as if the saints are actually watching us, as much as it means they have provided an example:

"It is not so much they who look at us as we who look to them—for encouragement."[1]

If you're in a situation where your loyalties are being questioned, think of Ruth, who left her homeland to embrace God's people. If you're facing a situation where you feel like standing up for righteousness may very well threaten you, think about Daniel in the lions' den or Esther as she approached the king, risking her own life in the process. Use the lives of past biblical characters to keep you on track, living on the edge for Jesus Christ.

"LET US RUN . . ."

I remember playing football and baseball in front of a crowd. Games are always different than practice, when people aren't watching. The fact that you have a crowd makes you want to do your best. In such situations, you certainly don't want to walk; you want to *run*.

Yet I see a lot of people trying to "walk" the Christian life instead of "run" it. They want to do the least amount of work, just to get by. Maybe they hope to just "squeeze" into heaven without anything to show for it. They've trusted Jesus for their salvation, but now live a self-absorbed life.

I hope that's not you. There's a radio station that uses this slogan: "Listen to 96.7 FM, the station that plays the music that makes your day go faster."

At first glance, there's nothing wrong with this slogan, until you realize the sadness behind it. Apparently, there are enough people who just want to "make it through the day" that a radio station specifically targets them with a message that promises to make the day go faster. These listeners are "wishing their lives away," coming in at 8:00 A.M. and already wishing it was 5:00 P.M.

I don't want my days to go fast because I love what I do. When I wake up on Monday, I don't groan because it's not Friday. I *love* Mondays.

When people come to work with no bigger aim than passing the day, they are walking through life, not running. Some of you might say, "Of course you like Mondays. If *I* were a recording artist, I'd like Mondays, too," but I know a lot of young kids who relish each day even while they are students.

For instance, I know teens at a Christian academy

here in Nashville who wake up on Monday morning and look at school as a great adventure. These kids are full of the Lord, eager to use each day to live for Him. They're pumped! They've embraced the love of God, and they've been changed; they have a zeal for life. They pray, "Thank You, God, for creating another day. What do you want me to do?"

There are other kids, many of them depressed, who don't feel good about themselves and who can't take their eyes off themselves. To them, school is torture. They just want the day to end. Avoiding pain and boredom is the sole aim of their life.

The kids who run through life have found a cause bigger than themselves. They may still struggle with a few issues, but their focus is on advancing God's kingdom. Jesus has captured their imagination, and they spend their best hours and the bulk of their thoughts giving themselves over to Him.

The greatest joy you can have in this life is pouring yourself out on behalf of someone else—"giving it away." It's not about you; it's about reaching out to others.

When my mom was eight years old, she watched as her mom left her and her brother and sisters on the doorstep. Each kid was sent to a different relative. The family was completely broken up until my grandfather remarried a few years later and gathered everybody back together.

It would have been easy for my mom to become bitter, angry, spiteful, and filled with hate. But she made a choice to focus on becoming a good mom herself rather than obsessing over the bad mom she had. Rather than running the same old record over and over in her mind (*How could my mom do that to me?*) she chose to make another promise: *I'll never let that happen to my kids.* She took a terrible thing and turned it around, using it for positive motivation to become a great mom.

She succeeded. My mom is phenomenal.

I don't know about all the challenges you face, but I do know that you can choose whether those challenges will bury you and make you walk through life, or whether you'll use them for inspiration so that you can run through life.

The choice is yours.

"WITH ENDURANCE . . ."

After years of putting together songs on my guitar, I finally finished one that I was convinced would be a top hit. This song would be my lifetime meal ticket, catapulting me to fame and fortune in Nashville. I was twenty-one years old, figured I had paid my dues, and now was ready to hit the big time.

Filled with confidence, I walked into a record publisher's office and played the song live, eager to get the song over so that we could discuss the financial terms. There was a long pause after I quit playing, and I imagined the publisher was trying to add up how much he was going to have to pay me to produce this incredible piece of music.

"It's okay," he said hesitantly, "but it needs some work."

I sat there in disbelief. *Okay? Needs some work?* Hadn't this guy just heard my all-time best song? What was the matter with him?

Walking out, I tasted the now all-too-familiar taste of rejection. Once again I had gotten my hopes up. Once again they were dashed against the rocks. I wasn't a teen anymore. How much longer could I go on? Was I just kidding myself?

I let myself hurt—for thirty minutes. I admitted I was disappointed, but a half hour later, I was already plotting my next song. I promised myself that I'd break into this crazy business somehow.

"Okay, Lord," I prayed, "I know You're in control, and You've allowed this to happen for a reason. I don't understand it, but I trust You."

Though I probably wouldn't have wanted to hear this then, now I know that there's nothing more character-building than disappointment. As much as I hated rejection, it made me a stronger and better person. Unfortunately, there are no shortcuts to Christian maturity. We can't take a pill or pop some "Christian vitamins" and expect to be changed overnight. God has to mold us, shape us, and transform us. Sometimes, that can be a pretty painful process.

You know what? You can do yourself a big favor by praying through each phrase in Hebrews 12:1. Remind yourself that you're living out your life in front of a great cloud of witnesses. Use that as motivation to run your life instead of walk through it. Be willing to endure the hardships you'll face, and promise yourself you won't stop until you get there. The only race you can run is the race that God places before you.

This really is your time. I pray that you'll make the most of it.

IN THE VIDEO for *This Is Your Time,* I think one thing comes out very clearly. Cassie's story *happened.* It is pure. It isn't some fantasy, some cooked-up Christian propaganda. I'm not trying to shove my views on anybody here; I'm just trying to tell a true story of a young woman who gave up her life for what she believed in.

Even if you're an atheist or a God-hater, you can't deny the fact that this is a pure thing. Some young people have been so committed to their faith, so sincere in their beliefs, so convinced of the reality of God in their lives, that they chose an early, violent death rather than deny the love they found in their souls.

Have you ever known that kind of love? Have you ever believed in something enough to be willing to die for it?

Cassie lived a hateful, bitter life until she gave her heart to Jesus Christ. I honestly believe that her life-change is even more inspiring than her death. The two years she lived as a Christian speak just as loudly as the few seconds in which she became a martyr.

May all of us consider the change that can come about when we give our hearts to God without holding anything back. None of us knows how much longer we have to live, or what tests God has in store for us, but one thing is certain: each one of us will face a moment when eternity whispers into our hearts, *This is your time.*

NOTES

Chapter 3

1. Excerpted from *She Said Yes* by Misty Bernall, Plough Publishing House, © Copyright 1999. Used by permission.

2. Bob Larson, *Extreme Evil: Kids Killing Kids* (Nashville: Thomas Nelson, Inc., 1999), 9–10.

Chapter 4

1. *Discipleship: Living for Christ in the Daily Grind*, by J. Heinrich Arnold, is published by Plough Publishing House, Route 381 North, Farmington, PAS 15437.
   For further information, call (800) 521-8011.

Chapter 5

1. Quote and information from Patricia Bosworth, "Kazan's Choice," *Vanity Fair*, September 1999, 324 ff.

2. Quote and information from Bruce Handy, "Return from Planet Pee-wee," *Vanity Fair*, September 1999, 346.

Chapter 6

1. "Kentucky Rose" written by Michael W. Smith and Wayne Kirkpatrick. © Copyright 1998 Milene Music, Inc. (ASCAP), Careers-BMG Music Publishing, Inc. (BMI), and Magic Beans Music (BMI). All rights on behalf of Magic Beans Music administered by Careers-BMG Music Publishing. All rights reserved. Used by permission. International rights secured.

Chapter 7

1. Excerpted from Bernall, *She Said Yes*, 83.
   Used by permission.
2. Ibid., 84.
3. Ibid., 93.

Chapter 9

1. Frank Deford, "Father Phil," *Sports Illustrated*,
   1 November 1999, 84.
2. Excerpted from Bernall, *She Said Yes*, 100.
   Used by permission.
3. Bruce Waltke, *Finding the Will of God*
   (Vision House Publishing, Inc., 1995).

Chapter 11

1. Craig Cabaniss, "Holy Fear: God Rules!"
   Sovereign Grace, January/February 1999, 4; c.f.
   www.pdinet.org.

Chapter 12

1. Tim Crothers, "Atlanta Thrashers," *Sports
   Illustrated*, 4 October 1999, 99.

Chapter 13

1. No author cited, *Sports Illustrated*,
   1 November 1999.
2. Excerpted from Bernall, *She Said Yes*, 103.
   Used by permission.
3. For more information about sponsoring
   a needy child, call Compassion International
   at (800) 336-7676.

Chapter 14

1. Erik Larson, *Isaac's Storm: A Man, a Time, and the Deadliest Hurricane in History* (New York: Crown Publishers, 1999); cited in W. Jeffrey Bolster, "Wall of Water," *The New York Times Book Review*, 12 September 1999, 46.

Chapter 15

1. Cited in David Bromwich, "Lincoln as We Know Him," *The New York Times Book Review*, 28 November 1999, 35.
2. Ibid.

Chapter 16

1. F. F. Bruce, *The Epistle to the Hebrews* (Grand Rapids, MI: Eerdmans, 1964), 346.